THE INSTITUTE OF PUBLIC AFFAIRS

THE UNIVERSITY OF VIRGINIA

# THE COUNTRY LIFE
# OF THE NATION

*The University of North Carolina Press, Chapel Hill,
N. C.; The Baker and Taylor Company, New York;
Oxford University Press, London; Maruzen-Kubushiki-
Kaisha, Tokyo; Edward Evans & Sons, Ltd., Shanghai.*

# THE COUNTRY LIFE
# OF THE NATION

BY

JAMES ERNEST BOYLE
CHARLES ERNEST ALLRED
LEON EDGAR TRUESDELL
ERNEST CHARLES YOUNG
EUGENE CUNNINGHAM BRANSON
BENJAMIN T. GUNTER
FLORENCE ELIZABETH WARD
JULIA D. CONNOR
EDGAR WALLACE KNIGHT
FANNIE WYCHE DUNN
NEWELL LEROY SIMS
JOHN HARRISON KOLB

EDITED, WITH AN INTRODUCTION, BY
WILSON GEE

CHAPEL HILL
THE UNIVERSITY OF NORTH CAROLINA PRESS
1930

## PREFACE

The Institute of Public Affairs was organized for the purpose of advancing the popular understanding of current public questions, economic, social, and political, through a study and discussion of those problems which are of immediate concern and interest to the American people.

From the beginning, a part of the program each year has been a round table on some phases of our country life problem because it has seemed to the Director and Board of Advisers that no question is more timely or so greatly in need of a satisfactory solution. Recent developments in the agricultural situation have only emphasized the predominant importance of the subject and the necessity for clear thinking and intelligent guidance in the formulation of a policy which will lead to an improvement in the present status of the farmer and provide a basis for a permanently prosperous agriculture.

Those persons who discussed the subject at the Third Session of the Institute were chosen because of their recognized leadership in the phase of the subject under consideration.

These discussions were of value to those who attended the round table meetings and those who read accounts of the meetings in the public press or obtained copies of individual addresses, but it was wisely suggested that because of the general excellence of the prepared papers, the proceedings merited publication in a more permanent form and, therefore, it was decided to publish this volume. This was made possible through the coöperation of the University of North Carolina Press.

The volume is sent forth in full confidence that it will make a real contribution toward the solution of one of the most urgent and difficult problems affecting our national welfare.

Grateful acknowledgment is made to those persons who contributed the papers which are included, to Dr. E. C. Branson, who assisted in preparing the program and directed the round table, and to Dr. Wilson Gee, who acted as secretary of the round table, and collected and edited the material herein presented.

CHAS. G. MAPHIS
*Director of the Institute*

# INTRODUCTION

## BY WILSON GEE

The farm industry of the United States has been ailing for the past decade or more. The other business interests of the nation, now passing through the inevitable slump in the business cycle, rather quickly recovered from the depression in the aftermath of the World War. Not so with the farming situation. While the status of agriculture has been somewhat improved in the past few years, the condition for the industry as a whole has been decidedly subnormal, accentuatedly so in recent months.

Various economists, agricultural leaders, farmers, politicians and others have in their own terms diagnosed the illness and prescribed widely different remedies. These range from the simple statement that farm relief is a matter of self-help on the part of the farmers to such complicated arrangements as the McNary-Haugen measure and the export debenture plan. The creation of a Federal Farm Board, and the giving to it of extensive powers and financial backing have created the hope that an able group of men may find ways successfully to meet a difficult and complicated situation. But the way this result is to be achieved has not yet been made clear.

The country life of this nation has always been a vital element in the greatness of our people. If the predictions of some of our closest students of population are correct, this is likely to be even more true in the future than in the past. We are told so rapidly is the city birth rate declining that with the increasing death rate which occurs in a citizenship of older age levels, there will evolve a stabilized population in the urban centres a generation from now. Immigration quotas remaining as at present, the cities will more largely than ever before depend upon the country for their growth. Such conditions already are operating to diminish proportionately the increase of the domestic demand for the products of the farm. It is to be hoped that our vast agricultural resources will become in the future years much more important in an export trade with less-favored nations than ours in the matter of agricultural produce for food, clothing and the raw materials of industry.

The fundamental importance of the American farm life problem calls for the serious questioning and planning for its relief on the part of all of our thoughtful citizenship, both rural and urban. Is there a safe basis for a permanently prosperous agriculture? Why are some sections of the nation such large farm wealth producers but so poor in the retention of farm wealth? How must an industrial development be planned to benefit mutually in the largest measure both manufacturing and agriculture? Are the changes taking place in the rural family wholesome in their ultimate effects upon that basic institution in our national life? What should be done to give equality of educational opportunity as between the country and the city child? To what extent is coöperative enterprise a solution of

the ills of agriculture? Country community life is un-
dergoing marked readjustments today. Are such changes
an improvement? Do our small towns measure up to
their obligations and opportunities towards their surrounding rural areas?

These are only a few of the many questions which
are considered in the following pages. An unusually
able group of men and women, specialists in their respective fields, discuss these matters for you out of their
years of rich experience. While perhaps no final
answers will be discovered, those who read this little
volume will find their interest kindled in the country
life of the nation, and their minds greatly enriched as
to what is happening in this important phase of American civilization. Such is the purpose of these round
tables in the Institute of Public Affairs.

Some final words of acknowledgment are necessary
and are gratefully made. The exacting duties as Secre-
tary of the Round Table on "The Country Life of the
Nation" have been made less burdensome through the
constant encouragement of Dr. Charles G. Maphis,
Director of the University of Virginia Institute of Public Affairs, and the efficient Secretary of the Institute,
Miss Eleanor D. Gibson. The associations with Dr. E. C.
Branson, Professor of Rural Social-Economics in the
University of North Carolina and Leader of this Round
Table, in the helpful conferences on its planning and
in his fine leadership in carrying out the program, con-
stitute pleasant recollections which can never be effaced.
Without the generous coöperation of the several
speakers in the preparation and delivery of their

addresses this volume would not have been possible. And fundamental to the success of the entire undertaking has been the fine audiences given by those who, in attendance upon the Institute, chose this Round Table for their especial interest. We hope in some measure, at least, that the stimulating atmosphere of these sessions in the East Room of Madison Hall in August of 1929 may be carried over to the wider audience reached by this attractive and meaty little volume.

# TABLE OF CONTENTS

\* Now deceased.

# I

# FACTORS IN THE RETENTION OF FARM WEALTH

# THE BASIS OF A PERMANENTLY PROSPEROUS AGRICULTURE

## BY JAMES ERNEST BOYLE

In facing the serious problems of our present farm life, we must frankly recognize the pertinent fact that we have evolved as a nation from the status of a rural democracy and an agricultural state to the status of an urban and industrial state. Fewer than one-fourth of our people now live on farms. This vast economic evolution has been due to one economic cause, namely, the fact that here in the United States six per cent of the world's population has fifty per cent of the world's basic industrial resources of iron, coal, copper, lead, zinc, petroleum, timber, and so on. This evolution, I repeat, is due to natural, not to artificial causes. We must go forward, not backward, in our economic life. We are not headed "peasant ward," to use that much abused word. In fact, peasants the world over are headed upward, not downward.

I have mentioned our economic evolution as one fact we must keep in our minds as a background of this discussion. There is a second fact which must form part of this same background, namely, the so-called "inequality of agriculture." As generally used this phrase has little or no validity. But, there is an economic inequality between agriculture and industry which must be recognized as fundamental, namely, the economics of raw material. The farmer is a producer of raw material. Studies of prices and price cycles show that prices of raw material fluctuate more than do the prices of finished goods. This is due to the simple fact that there is a quicker and better adjustment of supply to demand in the case of finished goods than there is with raw materials. For instance, if the baker finds too many loaves of bread on the market today he makes fewer loaves tomorrow. If the flour miller finds too much flour on the market this week, he makes less flour next week. But, if the farmer finds an oversupply of wheat on the market this year, it takes him another year to change the supply. For wheat once produced and reported by the Government is a market supply no matter whether it is stored on farms, at local elevators, or at terminal markets. Once produced its price influence is quickly registered, regardless of its location or rate of flow to market. To change its price it is necessary to change the supply actually produced, or, what amounts to the same thing, change the official estimate of the supply produced.

The farmer is a wholesaler of raw material; wholesale prices are the first prices to change; other prices, such as retail prices, wages, and salaries lag behind. Therefore, the economics of wholesale prices decrees that farmers are among the first to suffer in a falling market. No law of Congress can change this inequality of agriculture. This gives the farmer a disadvantage or inequality in a falling market. However, in a rising market, since wholesale prices go up first and farthest, the farmer has an advantage here exactly corresponding to his disadvantage on a falling market.

So much for the background of this discussion. In considering the factors in the retention of farm wealth we may well ask, what is the goal we have in mind?

## THE GOAL

The goal, as I see it, is a permanently prosperous agriculture, based on the family-sized farm. One would like to add the Biblical image of every man dwelling under his own vine and fig tree. But, whether the farmer is an owner, as in France, or a renter, as in England, it is possible to build up a class of prosperous farmers dwelling in a beautiful countryside. In other words, while our instincts shrink from tenancy, yet it may be both necessary and wise to have a high per cent of tenancy. Tenancy, in itself, is not bad although much and perhaps most of the tenancy in the United States is bad both for the land and for the tenant. The reform here may take the course of less tenancy or a better tenancy. This subject cannot be discussed further here for lack of time. The goal, whatever the form of land tenure, is, as stated before, a permanently prosperous agriculture on a family-sized farm. Stated more specifically, a prosperous agriculture means that the soil itself, as well as the man on the soil, must be conserved. The soil must be conserved against permanent destruction by erosion, and against the impairment of its fertility by whatever means. This is a basic fact in agriculture which is sometimes overlooked in our current discussions of "farm relief." A permanently prosperous agriculture means, further, that not merely is the farmer's physical plant, the soil itself, kept up, but also his capital, investment in buildings, and equipment. And finally, on top of these requirements of soil maintenance and capital investment is, of course, an income commensurate with the managerial ability, the labor, and the plant investment of the farmer. There is probably rather general agreement as to the goal I have described. But, there is certainly a lack of agreement as to the best roads to follow to reach this goal. As I see the problem, there are certain roads which are clearly wrong roads as there are others which are the right roads. We have now reached the point in this discussion where we may look into this question of the right or the wrong roads to the goal.

## Wrong Roads to the Goal

In the last few years of farm-relief discussion, many proposals for helping the farmer have been made. No doubt, some of these proposals have had great merit; some have had no merit; some have been harmful. If agriculture is to advance in an orderly and balanced manner, no one part of the industry should be promoted at the expense of any other part. We must keep in mind a balanced agriculture. Dairy farmers should not be torn down to build up the corn and wheat farmers. Cotton farmers should not be taxed to promote the hog farmers and so on. There are four or five proposals for helping agriculture which are, in my opinion, the wrong roads to the goal. For the sake of brevity it will be necessary to discuss these with a little more dogmatism than I like to employ.

1. *Corporation Farming.*—The suggestion has been made in many quarters that the farm be factoryized and that farms, like railroads, be run by corporations. The theory is simple: employ experts to use scientific methods; use power and machinery and get mass production. The theory is sound enough as a theory, but it does not work in practice. I divide all corporation farms into two classes: those which have failed; those which will fail. Farming is a small-scale business, needing constant and careful attention to details. There are differences of soils, of topography, and other factors on any one farm; farming does not lend itself to large-scale mass production methods.

2. *Cheap Credit.*—Cheap credit is undoubtedly a good thing for anyone capable of using it wisely. But, as has been said by other writers, credit is a two-edged sword. A wrong use of credit has bankrupted many a farmer. Cheap credit means dear land. The Federal Farm Loan Act was an important measure and helped many a farmer. But when it brought cheap land credit it thereby had a powerful influence in boosting land prices and stimulating the land boom in several of our States. It was aimed to help the weak farmer, but it was more generally used by the strong farmer. That is one reason the loan limit was changed from $10,000 to $25,000. This is not an argument against cheap credit. But it does show that cheap credit may hurt about as many as it helps. As the Germans found out in their coöperative schemes, guidance in the use of credit is fully as important as the securing of the credit itself.

3. *Protective Tariff.*—It has become difficult, if not impossible, to get the public interested in the merits of the tariff, the assumption being that a protective tariff protects and benefits the country as a whole and the various parts and divisions of the whole. I feel very sure that the best that can be truthfully said for the protective tariff is that it has speeded up a little the development of certain industries and enterprises that would have developed by themselves later if they were sound. Tariff tinkering goes on at Washington every four or five years, on the average; so the tariff basis is obviously a mere quicksand for a foundation for any permanent agricultural investments. The present method of building up tariff schedules on the so-called differences in cost of production at home and abroad has one serious defect among others: an increase in such a tariff, based on a cost of production survey, brings a few more high-cost producers into the field, this in turn raises the average cost of production once more above the foreign competition level and so justifies another increase in the tariff. And, just as inflation of an irredeemable paper currency breeds a new inflation, so one tariff increase soon calls for another increase. If we would put a tariff of $5.00 a bushel on wheat, we would actually increase the number of farmers who grow wheat at a loss.

It is my opinion that the tariff is now and always has been a very minor factor in the industrial growth of this country. It is in New England where the tariff medicine has been applied more and longer to industry, and it is exactly in New England where industry is now the sickest. The medicine has likely done the patient more permanent harm than good. Finally, we need more commerce, not less commerce, and the tariff is a very serious barrier to peaceful and healing commerce. The farmer's interests all lie in the direction of greater freedom of trade with all nations. The so-called pauper labor of the world is usually the dearest labor in the world. It was Henry Ford's highest priced labor in the world which made the cheapest car in the world.

4. *Government Bounties and Subsidies.*—Reliance on governmental bounties and subsidies to promote agriculture seems to me even more fallacious than depending on the tariff. The export bounty plan, advocated by certain of our citizens in recent months, has the added objection that it legally constitutes dumping and would therefore come into collision with the antidumping laws of practically all our foreign customers. In view of the fact that we have each year an exportable surplus of fifteen million tons of food, using an export bounty would be playing with economic dynamite.

A bounty or subsidy may be compared with a dole. A dole to American agriculture would be as demoralizing as the dole to British labor.

5. *Governmental Schemes of Price Control.*—This is neither the time nor the place to enter into a prolonged discussion of price control schemes, such as the Stevenson plan of rubber prices elevation in the East Indies, of sugar price control in Cuba, coffee valorization in Brazil, cotton price control in Egypt, and numerous other similar experiments. To the extent that they fail to control production they must fail to control prices. This fact seems so self-evident as to need no further evidence to

sustain it. The trouble with such remedies is that they leave the farmers worse off than they found them.

Enough time has been taken up in this purely negative part of my task. I turn now to the more pleasant duty of pointing out some constructive aspects of our problem.

### Right Roads to the Goal

Evidently the first point we can all agree upon is that we need a long-time program for agriculture. In looking over the twenty or thirty State production programs thus far formulated or discussed, I note but one State that is planning a fifty-year program. Big business is big largely because it does plan ahead and adopt policies accordingly. The Bell Telephone companies and the Anthracite Coal companies are two very good examples. In a certain coal engineer's office in Scranton, for instance, you will find maps on the wall covering the general plans of the company for the next one hundred years, and blue prints on the wall for the next fifty years of operations.

There is, as I have said elsewhere, not a plan but anarchy in our agriculture. It is indeed a three-fold anarchy which may be classified under the three heads: disorderly development, disorderly production, and disorderly marketing of perishable products. Any program for retaining our farm wealth must deal fundamentally with these three conditions.

Anarchy in development may be illustrated by the simple fact that in the decade ending in 1920, we plowed up grass lands and cut down forests and thus put into cultivation forty-five million acres of new land, most of which was not needed for crops. During the next five years thirty-one million acres of this forty-five million went back out of cultivation. No wonder the records showed an increase in farm bankruptcies. This was a tragic way to develop our agricultural plant. Obviously there is needed a national land policy governing the utilization of lands and the development of new lands. It is now quite generally agreed that no new irrigation projects are needed, but additional reforested areas are needed as well as new park and recreational areas, game and bird sanctuaries, and so on. Such a program of development would mean less land in farms, fewer farmers, and less competition among farmers. Presumably marginal and sub-marginal land would be put out of cultivation.

Anarchy in production may be illustrated by the over-planting of wheat and cotton under the temporary stimulus of war prices. The wheat acreage leaped upward 66⅔ per cent in two years. Cotton acreage jumped fifty-three per cent in four years. The increased production brought on the six-year discussion of "surplus control." The real trouble was surplus production, not surplus marketing. In tree crops, such as peaches and vineyards, we have seen similar examples of over-expansion in recent years. Here the problem of disorderly production is a more serious one than is the case with the annual crops, for it is harder to make the shift into and out of such farm enterprises. Of course, the weather is the factor of first importance in controlling size of output of most crops and the weather is not subject to human control. Nevertheless, much can be done by means of sound production policies to take some of the anarchy out of production, and to better adjust the production to consumer demand. Adjustment of production to consumer demand must include not merely the quantity but the quality wanted. For instance, the last report of our Secretary of Agriculture (1928) states that most of the cotton grown in the United States has a staple length of seven-eighths of an inch or less, but that this is not the staple demanded by most of the mills. If the roll is called of the various major farm crops and a check up is made as to their grade and quality and the grade and quality most in demand, it will be seen that a very poor adjustment of production to demand is now being made. Concerted action is needed to formulate production policies. Persuasion rather than compulsion is needed to get these policies carried into effect.

Anarchy in marketing is the least important of the three kinds of anarchy on the farm, but it is the one we have heard the most about. I wish to state emphatically that disorderly marketing is a serious problem only with our perishable crops and has no significance when applied to cotton and wheat. For cotton and wheat are stored at terminal markets for long periods; they are non-perishable; they are standardized and graded; they are traded in for future delivery. Hence the flow to market, the receipts at domestic market, the so-called dumping, have no effect whatever on price. The Minneapolis wheat market, for instance, absorbs one car of wheat, or ten, or a hundred, or a thousand, in a day with equal ease and lack of disturbance, because the quantity bought and paid for is hedged by sale for future delivery. The futures market is a very wide market. The dumping dogma has received such wide circulation that it is hard to convince some people even yet of its complete falsity. The term, orderly marketing, should be saved for our perishable fruits and vegetables and for livestock, fields where market gluts and market famines make the market price seesaw and cause the producer to get whipsawed. Why ship seventy-five cars of ripe peaches to Pittsburgh, when that market is asking for fifteen carloads? Why give New York City two hundred cars of ripe grapes when she asks for fifty? These perishable crops represent a business of a billion dollars a year, of which ten per cent, or a hundred million a year, is estimated to be the avoidable loss through disorderly marketing.

Here surely is a field for Industry Coöperation, for the formation of more clearing houses representing the different interests involved.

If what I have said about the three-fold anarchy on the farm is true, and I believe it is, then obviously definite policies of orderly development, of orderly production, and of orderly marketing of perishables will go far towards fundamentally strengthening our agriculture and retaining our farm wealth.

Thus far we have been looking into general principles. At this point in the discussion I desire to direct attention to the more specific aspects of the problem, or to what may be termed programs of action.

## Programs of Action

Men who agree on general principles of action usually differ and sometimes quarrel over programs. Our foreign diplomats frequently agree "in principle" to a proposition which they mean to oppose in practice. Hence, when I begin to specify particular programs of action, I am certain to be condemned for my sins of either omission or commission.

Eighteen years ago I was tremendously impressed by a certain statement made by Bradford Knapp before the First Annual Conference of the Bankers' Committees on Agricultural Development (1911). Dr. Knapp was speaking of mobilizing our existing knowledge and used these words:

The great problem of today is the dissemination of existing knowledge. That is true not only of Agriculture, but of almost every other human endeavor. If the existing knowledge with regard to human health were known and commonly practiced by the people generally, the ills of the human body would be much decreased. If the knowledge with regard to the best and most successful methods of conduct of farms were to become the common practice of the average farmer the agriculture of this country would be revolutionized. In every community, in every county, in every State you will find farmers who are making a distinct success of the business of farming; also, in every community you will find men who are merely scratching the surface of Mother Earth for a very poor existence.

Confirming what Dr. Knapp said in the year 1911 and introducing my own ideas on the subject, I want to insert at this point the results of the J. C. Neff "Study of forty-four Ohio farms as a basis of determining some factors of financial success in farming" (Cornell Thesis, 1927). Mr. Neff took the year 1925 for his study of the one hundred Ohio farmers with the most complete farm accounts. To make the picture more truly representative, the twenty-two farmers at the top of the list were selected and the twenty-two farmers at the bottom of the list. These forty-four were visited and interviewed, in addition to having their farm accounts analyzed. Here then was a cross-section of Ohio agriculture taken in a year of so-called farm depression and representing typical farmers scattered through seven counties of the State. The study showed in an impressive manner that farmers of about the same age, with about the same size farms, with the same climate and soil, the same markets, the same opportunities, differed nevertheless very widely in their financial success as farmers. The top man of the forty-four farmers had a labor income of $6,754, the bottom man of $81, a difference of over eight thousand per cent. The average labor income for the 22 top farmers was $3,368; of the bottom 22, $626. In other words, the top farmers of the hundred had an income 438 per cent larger than that of the bottom farmers.

This survey analyzes in great detail the economic and personal factors which account for these striking differences in income among farmers similarly situated and with the same opportunities and the same farm management problems. As Dr. Knapp pointed out, the problem is, how to make a better farmer out of the average individual farmer. The germs of success or failure

lie in him, rather than in outside factors or institutions.
Farm relief which merely changes the marketing system
is only playing with the surface of things. The problem
is far deeper than that. Farming is now a commercial
proposition, which means that the farmer produces most
of his stuff for the market and buys most of his requirements on the market. This new situation means, further-
more, that farming is not only competitive as never before, but that it is getting daily more competitive. Such
modern economic changes as the chain store, improved
refrigeration and storage, improved canning and processing, improved transportation, and so on, all add to
the competition which the farmer feels. Since competition is the price of progress, I doubt very much that
we ought to protect the farmer from this competition
by artificial barriers and screens. Better far to train him
to fight his battles. Important shifts in production have
been forced on the farmers in the past and will be in
the future. For instance, the main crop in the United
States now is the milk crop, being worth twenty-five dollars per capita, or two and a half times the cotton crop.
But when the process of manufacturing milk powder
is perfected, as it soon will be, it will completely revolutionize the whole milk market in every city in America,
and also, of necessity force drastic shifts in production
on the dairy farms in the high-cost sections of the East.
Agricultural statesmanship of a high order is needed
to foresee and prepare for these changes. Yes, farming
is now commercial and competitive.

I have already suggested that we need to mobilize existing agencies for helping agriculture. In my opinion

we have enough data on hand entombed in the vaults
at Washington or in cold storage at our state experiment
stations and agricultural colleges to revolutionize agriculture. We have enough agencies in existence to carry
this information to the individual farmers, if such
agencies could be mobilized.

### Mobilizing Existing Agencies

In mobilizing existing agencies for helping agriculture, the objective is, as I see it, primarily to help the
individual farmer become a better farmer by means of
self-help, and secondarily to promote group activity
where individual action is inadequate. Some of the major
agencies which are or can be mobilized for agriculture
are the following:

1. *Federal Farm Board.*—The newest agency of all
is, of course, the Federal Farm Board. At this stage of
its life it is impossible to say exactly what its powers
are or what it conceives its own duties to be. But, I would
venture the prophecy that its major successes will come
through mobilizing existing agencies rather than in
creating new ones.

2. *County Agent Movement.*—This movement has
within itself almost infinite possibilities for good to the
farmers. It was created primarily as an educational
agency to help the farmers help themselves. The further
it gets from this ideal and the deeper it gets into commercial activities the less good it will do the farmers.
The chain farm movement may be commended in this
connection, for it is in reality the application by business men or farmers of the County Agent idea to a

2.

smaller and privately financed district. Thus far its record is very encouraging.

3. *Four-H Club Work.*—The Boys' and Girls' club work seems to me the outstanding agency of greatest promise to American agriculture. This movement dignifies and exalts farming; it brings to the youth of the country scientific information in its most attractive dress. It appeals to the imagination as well as to the head.

4. *Other Agencies.*—One of the greatest agencies in the world for improving agriculture is the United States Department of Agriculture. With its laboratories, its accumulated data, and its personnel it ranks far above any similar institution in the world. If its powers could be mobilized quickly where needed, when needed, much good would result. Let us hope that our new Federal Farm Board will work extensively in and through this mighty agency.

The various agricultural colleges and experiment stations are in the position of having much valuable truth in their possession, but not being able to get this truth carried into practice very quickly. Means must be found for utilizing this truth more quickly where needed and when needed.

The American Bankers' Association, the State Bankers' Committees on Agriculture, the Key Bankers, all are standing by, waiting to help build a permanently prosperous agriculture.

The ten thousand coöperative associations offer a very promising field for carrying out programs of orderly development, production, and marketing. Since the marketing problem is ninety per cent solved on the farms, it is hoped that the coöperative marketing agencies will use their powers in improving production.

The five-hundred farm journals, the business corporations directly interested in farming (railroads, implement houses, mail order houses, fertilizer companies, millers, packers, and so on) are willing and anxious to do their bit, if they can be shown what their bit is.

In conclusion, let me add that whatever agencies are used and whatever programs are adopted for retaining farm wealth, we ought to aim at preserving the maximum of self-help and individual initiative, at conserving both the soil and the man on the soil. But if the man on the soil is properly trained for his job and has the ability now needed by a good farmer, he will take care of the soil.

# WEALTH RETENTION IN THE RURAL SOUTH

## BY CHARLES ERNEST ALLRED

The question under discussion is one of the main economic problems of the rural South, namely, the vast volume of farm wealth produced from year to year and the small share of it remaining in the hands of farmers on the farms. In other words, it is the problem of retaining a fair share of the wealth produced.

We shall not discuss the desirability of wealth-retention; that will be taken for granted. Neither shall we discuss the related problem of methods of increasing production or income. And, the approach to the question will be from the standpoint of wealth-retention by farmers *as a group*, rather than from the standpoint of the individual farmer.

### FARM WEALTH DEFINED

What do we have in mind when we speak of the retention of farm wealth? There are several forms of such wealth, if we consider wealth as being anything of value to the agricultural industry; for instance, we might include brains, brawn, skill, and technical training as part of the farm wealth. But in this paper we shall confine our consideration to material wealth in the form of land, goods, or money. Hence, when we speak of retaining farm wealth, we have in mind the retention of one or more of the following principal forms of material wealth:

1. The soil in a productive state.
2. The terraces, drains, and irrigation works.
3. The trees, both orchard and forest.
4. The houses, barns, and fences.
5. The equipment, both farm and household.
6. The livestock of all kinds, productive and work stock.
7. The crops and livestock products.
8. The operating capital.
9. The investments in stocks, bonds, notes, mortgages, and savings accounts.

It is a matter of common knowledge that in some areas nearly all the farmers have accumulated considerable property, while in other regions most farmers possess but little—though there are a few "well-fixed" farmers in nearly every region.

Why are Southern farmers as a rule poor today? Is it because they *receive* less income, or because they *retain* less of their income than is true in other sections? Or, have they suffered from an inherited handicap?

Each of these factors has played a part. For instance, the wealth of Tennessee farmers in 1900 was still considerably less than it was in 1860, forty years before, due to the tragic and heartbreaking condition in which our farm families were left at the close of the Civil War. But during this period many states were forging rapidly ahead in wealth accumulation.

According to the investigations of the National Bureau of Economic Research, in not a single one of the Southern states is the farm income per capita equal to the average for the country as a whole; in 1919, the United States average was $362 as compared with $192 in Tennessee, $275 in North Carolina, and $214 in Virginia.

But it is in the *retention* of wealth in the hands of farmers on the farms that we are especially interested in this discussion.

For the purposes of this study, we have chosen to use the farm *income* data, for the year 1919, in comparing the various counties and states, for the reason that farm commodity prices appear to have been more nearly uniform at that time. It will be seen readily that if the price of one commodity were unusually high, or low, as compared with the general price level of farm commodities, it would change the rank of the areas producing that commodity. But, in 1919, the depression had not started, and the price of all the principal commodities was good.

### LOW RETENTION IN THE SOUTH

That the farmers of the South are not *today* retaining, in their own hands, the wealth which they produce to anything like the extent that the farmers of some other sections are doing, is well illustrated by Table 1.

This table shows, for instance, that whereas the farmers of Iowa receive only about 18.5 per cent of the total income of all the people of the state, they have accumulated 39.1 per cent of the property values in that state; and, that while the farmers of Illinois receive only 7.7 per cent of the state's total income, they possess 14.7 per cent of the wealth of the state. An

TABLE 1

A. COMPARISON OF THE PERCENTAGE OF TOTAL STATE INCOME RECEIVED
BY FARMERS AND THE PERCENTAGE OF WEALTH POSSESSED BY THEM*

| STATE | Per cent of total *income* of the state received by farmers, 1920 | Per cent of total *wealth* of the state in hands of farmers, 1922 |
|---|---|---|
| U. S. average | 13.4 | 12.3 |
| Iowa | 18.5 | 39.1 |
| Illinois | 7.7 | 14.7 |
| Nebraska | 23.9 | 40.5 |
| Minnesota | 17.2 | 24.2 |
| South Dakota | 41.2 | 49.3 |
| Missouri | 14.0 | 16.9 |
| Indiana | 13.7 | 15.2 |
| Kansas | 27.8 | 28.4 |
| North Carolina | 36.6 | 14.6 |
| South Carolina | 38.1 | 16.5 |
| Alabama | 26.2 | 11.8 |
| Arkansas | 39.8 | 17.3 |
| Louisiana | 17.0 | 8.0 |
| Mississippi | 41.8 | 21.1 |
| Georgia | 28.7 | 14.7 |
| Tennessee | 25.5 | 14.8 |
| Viriginia | 22.4 | 12.4 |

*Based on investigations of National Bureau of Economic Research.

inspection of the table shows a somewhat similar situation in the other North Central states.

In the South, however, a very different situation is found. North Carolina farmers receive 36.6 per cent of the state's total income, but now possess only 14.6 per cent of the wealth of the state. Virginia farmers receive 22.4 per cent of the state's income, but now have only 12.4 per cent of the wealth; and Mississippi farmers, while getting 41.8 per cent of the state's income, have retained only 21.1 per cent of the wealth in their own hands. The figures for the other Southern states show a similar situation to exist in each of them.

## Effects of Four Factors

*On Local Areas.*—In Table 2 an attempt is made to show the effects of four of the principal factors in farm wealth retention on the accumulation of property by farmers, using Tennessee counties as illustrations. These factors are fertility of the soil, diversification, white population ratio, and industrial development.

Thirteen groups of counties have been selected, each group representing a different combination of the above factors. The first column of figures shows, for the counties of each group, the ratio between the retention or accumulation of farm property and the income of the farmers. For instance, it is shown that in Chester County, Tennessee, the amount of wealth per farm is only 2.8 times as much as the annual *net* income of the farmers per farm.[1] For reference purposes the basic figures of net income per farm, and value of property per farm, have for each county been included in the table.

Group I (Chester, McNairy, Hardeman, and Fayette counties) is an area low in fertility, is a one crop (cotton) section, has a high negro ratio, and with no nearby industrial development to provide a market for surplus produce and to furnish outside work for some members of the family. In this area, the ratio of wealth to income is only a little over three to one. The average net income

---

[1] Net income is found by deducting from the gross income the value of feed fed, feed purchased, fertilizers, labor, interest on mortgage, and maintenance.

TABLE 2

THE EFFECT OF FOUR FACTORS ON THE RETENTION OF FARM WEALTH
IN TENNESSEE COUNTIES

| Groups of Tennessee Counties | Number of times farm wealth is of annual net farm income | Net farm income per farm, 1919* | Value of farm property per farm, 1920 |
|---|---|---|---|
| GROUP I | | | |
| Poor, one crop (cotton), high in negroes, no city influence: | | | |
|     Chester | 2.8 | $1,044 | $2,874 |
|     McNairy | 3.0 | 890 | 2,641 |
|     Hardeman | 3.3 | 903 | 2,934 |
|     Fayette | 3.3 | 897 | 2,924 |
| GROUP II | | | |
| Poor, one crop (corn), white, no city influence: | | | |
|     Pickett | 3.6 | 536 | 2,001 |
|     Fentress | 3.7 | 551 | 1,832 |
| GROUP III | | | |
| Medium fertile, one crop (tobacco), negroes, no city influence: | | | |
|     Montgomery | 2.8 | 1,532 | 4,351 |
| GROUP IV | | | |
| Medium fertile, one crop (tobacco), white, no city influence: | | | |
|     Macon | 3.5 | 886 | 3,085 |
|     Dickson | 3.7 | 910 | 3,307 |
| GROUP V | | | |
| Fertile, one crop (cotton) high in negroes, no city influence: | | | |
|     Lake | 2.9 | 3,220 | 9,152 |
| GROUP VI | | | |
| Medium fertile, one crop (corn), white, no city influence: | | | |
|     Jackson | 4.7 | 892 | 4,202 |
|     Clay | 4.9 | 644 | 3,092 |

*Net income figured by method recommended by National Bureau of Economic Research.

TABLE 2—*Continued*

THE EFFECT OF FOUR FACTORS ON THE RETENTION OF FARM WEALTH
IN TENNESSEE COUNTIES

| Groups of Tennessee Counties | Number of times farm wealth is of annual net farm income | Net farm income per farm, 1919* | Value of farm property per farm, 1920 |
|---|---|---|---|
| GROUP VII |  |  |  |
| Medium fertile, diversified, white, no city influence: |  |  |  |
| Humphreys | 5.0 | $1,043 | $5,087 |
| Warren | 5.3 | 652 | 3,846 |
| White | 5.4 | 767 | 4,029 |
| GROUP VIII |  |  |  |
| Fertile, diversified, white, small city influence: |  |  |  |
| Greene | 6.5 | 868 | 5,667 |
| Blount | 6.7 | 968 | 6,390 |
| Maury | 7.4 | 1,185 | 8,728 |
| GROUP IX |  |  |  |
| Fertile, diversified, white, medium city influence: |  |  |  |
| Wilson | 8.1 | 832 | 6,684 |
| Williamson | 8.2 | 1,069 | 8,555 |
| Sullivan | 8.0 | 806 | 6,305 |
| GROUP X |  |  |  |
| Medium fertile, one crop (cotton), negroes, large city influence: |  |  |  |
| Shelby | 6.8 | 804 | 5,376 |
| GROUP XI |  |  |  |
| Poor fertility, diversified, white, large city influence: |  |  |  |
| Hamilton | 7.1 | 838 | 5,805 |
| GROUP XII |  |  |  |
| Medium fertile, diversified, white, large city influence: |  |  |  |
| Knox | 8.6 | 831 | 6,907 |
| GROUP XIII |  |  |  |
| Fertile, diversified, white, large city influence: |  |  |  |
| Davidson | 11.0 | 1,017 | 10,832 |

Economic Research.

*Net income figured by method recommended by National Bureau of per farm for this area is $933 per year, but the wealth accumulated per farm is only $2,843. This forms a striking contrast with Group XIII (Davidson County) which has fertile land, diversified farming, white population, and nearby industrial development. In the latter group the ratio of wealth to income is eleven to one; and, while the net income per farm is only $84 more per year than in Group I, the accumulation of wealth per farm is $10,832, or almost three times that of Group I.

An inspection of the table shows that between these two extremes there are many variations. For instance, Group V (Lake County) is the most fertile area of the entire state, but one cropping (cotton), a high negro ratio, and no industrial development cause the wealth retained by the farmers of that area to be only 2.9 times that of their annual net income. And in Group III (Montgomery County), although the soil is of medium fertility, the one crop system (tobacco), the high negro ratio, and no city development have caused wealth retention to be only 2.8 times the annual net income.

And, in this connection, it should be mentioned that cotton and tobacco are not the only one crop systems which affect wealth retention. Group II (Pickett and Fentress), the one crop corn area, shows an accumulation of only about 3.6 times its anual net income.

The fertile, diversified, white areas of the state are well illustrated by Groups VIII and IX. Group VIII (Greene, Blount, and Maury) which has only small city influence, has a retention ratio of about 6.9; while Group IX, with larger city influence, has a ratio of 8.1.

The contrast between the areas adjacent to the four large cities and showing the influence of fertility, diversification, and white population, is brought out in Group X (Shelby), XI (Hamilton), XII (Knox) and XIII (Davidson). While Memphis in Group X is the largest city of the four, the one crop system and the large number of negroes hold the retention ratio down to 6.8. Poor fertility keeps the Chattanooga area (Group XI) from going above 7.1. In the Knoxville area (Group XII), with medium fertility, the retention ratio rises to 8.6; while in the Nashville area (Group XIII), with all four factors favorable, the ratio rises to 11 to 1.

*On States and Regions.*—Having established these principles as they apply to different sections of Tennessee, it is pertinent to inquire as to whether or not they are applicable to the entire country. Table 3 throws some light on this subject.

Group I, consisting of the Southern states of Alabama, Arkansas, Mississippi, Georgia, South Carolina, and North Carolina, has a retention ratio of about 3.1 as compared with an average ratio for the whole United States of 7.2. Group I is an area of relatively poor soil, one crop farming, many negroes, and small city influence.

Group II, consisting of Tennessee, Virginia, and Kentucky, with somewhat more fertile soils, more diversity, and fewer negroes has a ratio of about 5.5.

Group V, embracing Iowa, Illinois, Indiana and Missouri, with rich soil, diversified farming, few negroes, and medium city influences, has an average retention

## TABLE 3

The Effect of Four Factors on the Retention of Farm Wealth
in the United States

| Groups of States | Number of times farm wealth is of annual net farm income | Net farm income per farm, 1919* | Value of farm property per farm, 1920 |
|---|---|---|---|
| GROUP I Poor soil, one crop (cotton), many negroes, small city influence: | | | |
| Alabama | 2.8 | $ 949 | $2,698 |
| Arkansas | 3.4 | 1,162 | 3,974 |
| Mississippi | 3.6 | 1,008 | 3,646 |
| Georgia | 3.3 | 1,338 | 4,366 |
| South Carolina | 2.9 | 1,712 | 4,946 |
| North Carolina | 3.2 | 1,454 | 4,634 |
| GROUP II More fertile, more diversity, fewer negroes, small city influence: | | | |
| Tennessee | 5.1 | 962 | 4,953 |
| Virginia | 5.7 | 1,119 | 6,425 |
| Kentucky | 5.8 | 968 | 5,587 |
| GROUP III Poor soil, diversified, few negroes, large city influence: | | | |
| Connecticut | 10.5 | 953 | 10,019 |
| Massachusetts | 10.3 | 913 | 9,389 |
| Rhode Island | 10.3 | 797 | 8,238 |
| GROUP IV Poor soil, diversified, few negroes, medium city influence: | | | |
| Vermont | 6.0 | 1,280 | 7,661 |
| New Hampshire | 7.1 | 811 | 5,782 |
| GROUP V Rich soil, diversified, few negroes, medium city influence: | | | |
| Iowa | 13.4 | 2,985 | 39,941 |
| Illinois | 10.6 | 2,657 | 28,108 |
| Indiana | 8.1 | 1,834 | 14,831 |
| Missouri | 9.1 | 1,504 | 13,654 |
| United States as a whole | 7.2 | 1,682 | 21,235 |

*Net income based on investigations of National Bureau of Economic Research.

ratio of 10.3; while in the state of Iowa it rises to 13.4 to 1.

New England affords a striking illustration of the effects of industrialization. Group III, consisting of Connecticut, Massachusetts, and Rhode Island, has a retention ratio of about 10.4, while the more remote states of Vermont and New Hampshire have a ratio of about 6.5. It is interesting to note in this connection that although the soil is poor and rocky in New England, yet the ratio of retention in most of it is much higher than in the South.

Maine, however, is quite different from the other New England states, and affords a good illustration of the principles set forth above. There is but little urban influence, the soil is poor and rocky, and diversity but little practiced. This set of circumstances leads to a retention ratio of only 3.7.

## OTHER FACTORS IN RETENTION

The writer is far from holding the opinion, however, that the four factors mentioned above are the only ones affecting wealth retention in the hands of farmers. He believes them to be some of the most important factors, and has attempted so to demonstrate in the foregoing. But there are many other factors, some of them objective and some of them subjective. It is fortunate that this is so; for, in many cases, it would be next to impossible for the individual farmer working alone to change all of the four factors mentioned above and at the same time remain in his present community. But, fortunately, there are a number of important factors that the farmer can change by himself; and by coöperative effort with other farmers he can change still more factors, the sum of which will bring prosperity to almost any area.

The writer has not the space to discuss in full each of these additional factors which would prove helpful in farm wealth retention, and will have to content himself with merely listing some of the more important of them, with a word of comment in a few instances:

1. Prevention of wastes on the farm from soil erosion, leaching of manure, unpainted, uncovered, and unrepaired buildings, fences, and machinery, etc.

2. Improvements in taxation and government, in the form of consolidation of poor counties; more efficiency and less graft in county government; larger state subsidies for schools, roads, county agents, home agents, vocational teachers, health units, sanitary officers, etc.; elimination of the state tax on general property, and the substitution therefor of a sales tax on tobacco, malt, gasoline, soft drinks, chewing gum, theatre admissions, etc.

3. Prevention of unwise purchases, such as unsafe stock selling schemes; articles sold by agents at above real value; unneeded, or unsuitable machines, tractors, silos, automobiles, etc.; food and feed which can be grown on the farm; fuel which the farm might supply; winter vegetables which a winter garden would provide; fertilizer when manure and legumes would do as well.

4. Cultivation of the ability to say *no*, to resist agents and salesmen, advertising appeal, temporary desires, and requests of children.

5. Eliminating or decreasing loss of wealth from pests, such as rodents, insects, plant and animal diseases, weeds, etc.

6. Conserving wealth in forests by preventing fires, caring for young trees, and using waste wood.

7. Conserving products by better storage facilities, on farms, at shipping points, and at terminals.

8. A greater use of by-products of farms, such as corn-stalks, wheat straw, weeds, etc.

9. Prevention of human disease, with its large cost in money, time, reduced efficiency, and decreased ambition.

10. Conserving the sales value of farm lands, by good roads, good schools, good neighbors, preventing negroization of the area, attractive appearance, telephone system, social organizations, favorable publicity, and the encouragement of industrial development, etc.

11. Inducing well-to-do farmers to retire on the farms, instead of in towns, cities, or other states.

12. Reducing bank failures and consequent heavy losses, by minimum standards, and careful inspection. This would also prevent money being sent north for deposit.

13. Coöperative selling, by means of which farmers would perform additional functions and be paid for it; produce better products; reduce selling expense; and broaden their markets.

14. Coöperative purchasing of farm and household equipment and supplies.

15. Coöperative use of farm equipment of a type which is expensive to purchase and seasonal in use.

16. Coöperative or mutual insurance, thus reducing cost of coverage for fire, windstorm, hail, automobile, life, sickness and accident, and annuity insurance.

17. Temperance in all things, including whisky, gambling, tobacco, luxurious foods, luxurious clothing, joy rides, etc.

18. Increased use of weather reports, to reduce losses from frost on fruits, rain damage to hay, etc.

19. Elimination of merchant credit, which now costs farmers huge sums each year.

20. A better form of tenancy, which would encourage a better class of tenant farmers.

21. Creation of a desire for a competence, in contrast with immediate consumption, and reduction in the effort to "keep up with Lizzie," by means of education in thrift.

22. Reduce shiftlessness and loafing, both white and black, by the elimination of certain diseases (such as hookworm, malaria, etc.) and by increasing human desires.

23. Increasing industrial development in small towns in agricultural districts, thus enabling some members of farm families, while living on farms, to earn money with which to pay their own expenses, and thus conserve the income from the farm.

24. The marrying by farmers of wives who will be true helpmeets, or partners in an economic sense, and not merely "helpeats."

25. The keeping in touch with the agricultural outlook reports, and adjustments of farming so that a produce will not be raised only to be wasted through lack of a market.

26. Less elaborate funerals in some cases, with their large money cost and loss of time.

27. Good physicians close at hand, to reduce expense of medical service, and increase human efficiency through more extensive use of such service and consequent better health.

28. The use of the *public* schools, by the sons and daughters of farmers, rather than attending the expensive private schools which are often no better adapted to their needs.

29. Reduction in the high rate of accidents on farms, with attendant expense, and loss of time and efficiency.

30. Protection against natural cataclysms such as floods, drought, etc.

31. Possibly a reduction in the size of families on farms with a consequent reduction in the cost of bearing, food, clothing, education, etc., since under present conditions children have become an economic liability.

### Conclusions

In the foregoing we have attempted to throw some light on why it is that most of the farmers in some areas have retained but little wealth; why and how a few farmers in each of the low-retention areas have accumulated a fair amount of property; and why nearly all farmers in some areas are "well-fixed."

The situation is not at all a hopeless one for the low-retention farmers of the South today. They have suffered severely in the past from the after-effects of the Civil War; from the economic bedlam which followed the liberation of the negroes; from distance to market; from high negro ratios; and from over-populated farms. But now the setting is changing. Industry is coming in;

diversification is being increased; negroes are leaving the farms for occupations better suited to their talents; and the fertility of the soil is being increased. These factors, and others that could be mentioned, are favorable omens, and we believe that the coming decades will see a rapid increase in wealth-retention by Southern farmers, until our farmers compare most favorably with those of any other section of the country.

# II

# THE CITYWARD DRIFT
# OF COUNTRY POPULATIONS

# THE EXTENT AND SIGNIFICANCE OF
# FARM MIGRATION

## BY LEON EDGAR TRUESDELL

One outstanding feature of the population statistics
of the past half century is the rapid increase in the proportion of the population living in cities and following
occupations other than agriculture. This is true not only
in the United States but in nearly all other civilized
countries. In 1880 less than three-tenths (28.6 per cent)
of our own people lived in urban territory (that is, in
cities and other incorporated places having 2,500 in-
habitants or more), and more than seven-tenths (71.4
per cent) in rural territory. In 1920 more than half the
population (51.4 per cent) was urban and less than
half (48.6 per cent) was rural.

In 1920 the population living on farms, counted sep-
arately for the first time in that year, formed not quite
three-tenths of the total. Since 1920 the farm population
has declined in absolute numbers from 31,000,000 to
probably not more than 27,500,000, which is considerably less than one-fourth of the estimated total population. The urban population, during the same period, has
increased by something like 20,000,000.

The average annual decrease since 1920 in the number of persons on farms has amounted to about 350,-
000. But if there were no migration from the farms,
the farm population would increase at least 400,000 a
year through the excess of births over deaths. It is evi-

dent, then, that the net migration from the farm to the city must be around 750,000 per year, or people enough to make a new city almost as large as Baltimore.

Fifty or sixty years ago the most important movement of our people was from the farms of the eastern and central sections of the United States to newer lands farther west. This movement, though, involved only the transfer of agricultural people from one section, to be agricultural people in another section. Frontier conditions were different, to be sure, but not radically different. The pioneer farmers were still farmers. The surplus farm population which now goes to the cities, however, finds not only a new place of residence but a new occupation and unfamiliar living conditions and social environment.

Why do three-quarters of a million people leave the farms every year for the city? Who are they that go? And what are the social consequences of their going?

There are superficial reasons for this movement which have often been discussed, though sometimes with more feeling than logic. Young men and young women brought up on the farm are attracted, it is said, by the glitter and excitement of the city; or they wish to escape the long hours and humdrum occupations of the country. Hence they seek employment in the city.

The cityward movement includes not only young people just leaving the paternal home, who simply take up an urban occupation as their first independent work, but also mature men who have spent many years in agriculture, who move to the city with their families and undertake new kinds of work under new conditions.

These men, too, are seeking an easier way of making a living, perchance, or more excitement or better schools for their children or any of a dozen so-called "advantages" of city residence.

But the reasons for the present wholesale transfer of population from the farms to the cities run deeper than these matters of personal preference or temporary advantage. There are three fundamental and far-reaching economic changes which make such a transfer almost inevitable.

First in point of time, and perhaps most important, is the development of factory production and the system of distribution which makes large-scale production possible. The early stages of this movement are often referred to as the "industrial revolution"—though perhaps the early readjustments were no more revolutionary than some which our present time requires. The coming of the factories created the industrial cities and added vast industrial populations to cities already existing. It likewise took out of the homes of the rural families a large amount of handicraft work and thus made these families almost entirely dependent on agriculture for a livelihood. First, income-producing crafts like weaving were transferred to the factories; and later even the processes of making goods for home consumption— spinning, knitting, sewing, and baking —have one after another followed suit.

One result of this movement has been to take the farmer farther and farther away from the old self-sufficing economy and bring him into a money economy, under which he produces stuff to be sold for cash, and with the cash buys most of the things he needs.

Every stage of this process results in the transfer of work-to-be-done from the farm to the factory—which usually means to the city. Let us take a specific example. In the olden days men on the farm cut logs and split rails out of which to build fences. Now the farmer buys fence wire and probably fence posts also, and in a few days puts up as much fence as would have resulted from weeks of labor under the old methods. In this case some of the labor is simply transplanted from the farm to the factory where the wire is made; and men are required there who would not be required if farmers were not using wire for fences. In other words, much of the farm work of our grandfathers' day is in effect done in a factory, just as the spinning and weaving of the colonial household are now done in the textile mill. And with the removal of the work has gone—and must go—the removal of enough men and women to do the work.

In so far as this change from local manufacture to centralized factory production has operated to transfer people from the farm to the city, it has taken the form of a direct call for workers to perform new tasks, or tasks undertaken under new conditions.

A second reason for the transfer of farm folk to the cities is the improvement in the processes of farming and in the organization of the agricultural industry. Machinery has been introduced for doing things that were formerly done by hand; first horse-drawn equipment and then that driven by mechanical power. The hoe, which has stood for ten thousand years as a symbol of the drudgery of agricultural labor, has very largely given way to machines and implements which perform the work of cultivation far more rapidly and far less laboriously.

New varieties of the standard crops have been introduced whose yield is double that of some of the old types. Specialization has been developed, under which a locality benefits to the full from the production of those crops which it can produce to best advantage. Thus cantaloupes are shipped from the Imperial Valley all over the United States, in spite of the fact that there is hardly a county in which cantaloupes can not be grown for the local market.

All of these developments, each one profitable to the individual farmer who takes advantage of it, make it possible for a stated quantity of farm products to be turned out by a smaller number of men. To feed a given population, then, under these new conditions, will require a smaller percentage of that population on the farms.

To a limited extent the export market may be developed to take care of the excess product of increasing farm efficiency. But exports can be disposed of, over a long period, only by taking imports in exchange for them. And in a country with such varied products as ours, there is a limit to the quantity of goods that can be freely imported without protest from those with whose production such imports may compete. Further, a country with a relatively high price level is not in a favorable position to dispose of standard commodities, like farm products, in the international market.

Unlike the concentration of machine production in factories, which seems to have reached nearly the limit to which it can profitably be carried, there is reason to expect much further advance in farm efficiency. For only a few farmers have so far taken advantage of all that science has done for agriculture, and there is room for great improvement through better training and better organization for those who now fall short of what the model farmers have demonstrated is practicable.

Under present conditions a surplus of farm products above what the domestic market will absorb at satisfactory prices is an outstanding factor in the farm problem. In fact, the agricultural surplus seems to be such a serious matter that some of the agencies for spreading the gospel of better farming are holding back, marking time, ready to renew their efforts as soon as the danger of pulling prices down through increasing the output has been taken care of.

The expansion of factory production, as we have seen, has drawn men off the farms into the cities by offering them attractive or profitable employment. The improvement in agricultural technique accomplishes the same result in a different way. It tends rather to push men off the farms by making it possible for an ever smaller number to produce all of the farm products for which there is demand.

A third reason for the transfer of workers from the farms to other places of activity grows out of the rising standard of living. The distribution of our working population among the various occupations will follow rather closely the demand for goods and services; and

with a rapidly rising standard of living there is bound
to be a change in the relative importance of the different
demands. The new things that are being added, year by
year, to the American standard of living are almost
without exception factory products rather than farm
products. Automobiles, radio sets, victrolas, electric
lights, telephones, household machinery, up-to-date
clothing—all these are made in city factories. The rapidly expanding "service occupations"—automobile service, hotel service, etc.—are likewise for the most part
city occupations. Hence as more of our people are able
to supply themselves with the new comforts and conveniences, there will be more demand for urban products
and urban workers. The demand for farm products, however, will increase only with the slow growth of population. In fact, the demand for food is increasing hardly
as fast as the population; for now that men do less of
heavy manual labor, they require less food per capita.

Farm products, except for cotton and tobacco, are
primarily things to eat. And as people spend a smaller
and smaller fraction of their total incomes for things
to eat, it would appear that a constantly decreasing fraction of the total number of workers need spend their
time in producing food.

The changing standard of living, then, like the expansion of the factory system, operates directly to draw
people off the farms by creating a demand for their
services in non-agricultural production.

So far we have assumed that the people who live
on the farms are, and will be, mainly engaged in farming as a means of livelihood and that they make up by

far the larger part of the total population living in the country. The number of families who live on places that are called farms, but do no farming, has been increasing rather rapidly, however, in the past decade. Especially in the New England and Middle Atlantic states do we find numerous cases where a man, employed in some city or town factory, has found it profitable to purchase a farm as a place of residence, and to travel each day by automobile the necessary two, or five, or even ten miles between the farm and the factory. This particular condition is mainly a temporary one, however, the result of a lower current price for farms (that is, for farm houses with a farm thrown in for good measure) than for city or village residences. The significant thing, from the point of view of country residence, would be the extensive building of new homes for city workers in the open country.

There is doubtless a growing tendency for city workers to live in the suburbs. Opinions differ widely as to its extent and we have no very satisfactory statistics by which to measure it. Personally, I am inclined to think that the extent of this development, up to the present time, has been over-estimated. Apartment houses are still going up rapidly in our larger cities, and much of the so-called suburban development takes the form of a continuous building up of the city, running across the nominal lines which mark the corporate limits. Residents in such a suburb live in the edge of the city, not in any real sense in the country.

Let us consider now some of the results of the transfer of people from the country to the city. One of the fortunate (but little appreciated) consequences of the movement of population off the farms is the present approach to a balance among the different lines of production. There is even now a surplus of many farm products, but this surplus would be larger if the 7,500,000 people who have left the farms since 1920 had all remained and added to the aggregate output.

There is a certain amount of unemployment in the cities, which might indicate that they were finding it difficult to provide occupation for all those who came in from the farms and elsewhere. At any given time, however, a considerable number of men will be out of employment because they are in process of going from one job to another; and it is only in a few cities and in a few declining industries that the number of unemployed is greatly in excess of the number of men who might reasonably be considered in such a transition stage.

But let us try to imagine what would happen if 2,000,000 or 3,000,000 workers were suddenly sent back to the farms to find jobs. We must certainly grant that there would then be far more serious unemployment on the farms and among these men than is now found in any urban center.

This maintenance of an approximate balance between production and demand is without doubt the most important of the consequences of the farm-city movement, from the economic point of view. The changing demand has been largely responsible for the transfer of workers, and this in turn has enabled production to meet the new demands.

Another effect of the demand which industry has made for the rural labor supply has been to stimulate more efficient methods in agriculture, especially a more efficient use of labor on the farm, whether through the use of additional machinery or through better organization. The farmer who wishes to hire labor is likely to be in direct competition with the industrial employer. This competition he must meet by offering higher wages and accepting shorter hours; hence he is obliged to make more effective use of such labor through a rearrangement of his working program.

In those matters which affect the country as a whole, the consequences of the movement of population from the farm to the city carry little cause for regret. It is otherwise with many local areas. There are communities which have lost the major part of their population in this way. There are townships in which the abandoned farms far outnumber the farms under cultivation. These are of course areas in which the farm land is not of the best quality—areas of marginal or submarginal land. The economist might declare that this land ought never to have been made into farms, even under the more favorable market conditions of pre-railroad days. But the effect of the loss of population on the social activities of the community is none the less serious.

Further, the migration from the farm to the city, especially that made up of young people just starting in life, is selective in its nature. It is largely the more enterprising young men who leave the farms and the less enterprising who stay. Many rural communities are thereby left without leaders and without material out of which to make leaders. This situation is most acute in those sections of the country where farming is less profitable and where there are prosperous and growing industrial centers. Such areas are numerous in New England and New York and there are some, I am sure, in your southern states.

I suppose that the migration of the southern negroes to the northern industrial cities has been of the same character; that is, it has taken the more enterprising of the colored laborers and has left the less enterprising. At any rate the colored workers one finds in a city like Chicago or Detroit seem to be more intelligent and more capable than the average of the colored laborers we have in Washington, D. C., who probably represent what might be termed the "run of the mine."

So far I have been trying to describe what has actually happened in connection with the migration of several millions of people from the farms to the cities, though perhaps my statements with regard to the selective nature of this migration contain some elements of personal opinion.

May I add a bit more of personal opinion in suggesting what might be the ideal or desirable distribution of workers, as between agriculture and urban industries? It seems to me that in general the least effective of the workers—those of the least intelligence and the least initiative—should work in the city factories, where they will perform very simple tasks under close supervision; that the most efficient individuals—those with capacity for leadership—should be employed in the city where they will have opportunity each one to direct the activ-

4

ities of many other workers; and that out of the inter-
mediate class should be selected as many as are needed
for work on the farms, where success requires more
initiative than in the majority of factory jobs, and where
the rewards are adequate for a moderate degree of
managerial skill.

One other factor should enter into this ideal selective
scheme. There is here and there a man of the highest
type who has such a natural love for the land that he will
prefer to remain on the farm, even though some other
occupation might offer greater financial returns. It is
from among these men, for whom Dr. C. J. Galpin has
coined the term "land-minded," that many of our future
rural leaders will come.

There is a large group of new social and economic
advantages enjoyed by the farmers of the present day,
some of which are the direct result of the migration of
a considerable part of the farm population to the city,
and some of which are incidental results of the general
prosperity of our nation. Where some of the members
of a farm family are engaged in city occupations, while
others remain on the farm, there is bound to be an exchange of ideas and opinions which broadens the outlook of the farm workers. By this means much of the
traditional conservatism of the farmer is being broken
down—though many other factors contribute to this same
end.

Partly because of the scarcity of labor, the farmer is
doing his work more with machinery. This means that
his occupation is fast becoming similar in many respects
to that of the man who operates a machine in a city

factory or shop. This is only one of a large number of conditions which tend to make the farmer more like the city worker and less in a class by himself. The automobile, which makes it easy for the farmer to visit the city at frequent intervals, is probably the most important single factor contributing to this tendency.

Other social tendencies might be enumerated, if time permitted, some of which indicate an inclination to transplant urban conveniences and urban customs into the country, while others represent a conscious effort to build up a strictly rural social structure and to preserve a feeling of unlikeness in the minds of the rural population.

We must not leave the subject, however, without saying a few words about the consequences of rural-urban migration for the individual who migrates. Let us ask, finally, then, what is the effect on the people who go from the farms or from other rural homes, of their change in residence and occupation?

They soon cease to be rural people—all but the most persistently land-minded of them—and become city people. This means, among other things, that they crowd more of activity and experience of some sort, if not of accomplishment, into each week or month that passes. They meet more people, though it is possible that they may have fewer friends. They are likely to live in rented houses, to move frequently, not only from one house to another but even from one city to another; hence they will not acquire that deep affection for a place called home which a rural family often has. The few who are inclined to read or to study will probably read more, partly because books and libraries are accessible and partly because the city resident gets into the habit of doing things faster; those who are inclined to unprofitable activities will likewise pursue these with more energy—and with a more rapid reaping of the consequences.

The children of the farm-bred men who have gone to the city will miss the "natural" environment of the country; and because cities are primarily constructed for grown-ups and not for children there will be appreciably fewer children in their families. For the rank and file—for those who perform routine tasks under supervision—life in the city will contain more experiences, though possibly not more of things that are really of permanent and lasting value. Incidentally, they will lose some of the initiative and resourcefulness which they had, or which might have developed if they had stayed in the country; but a man having little of these qualities may well be happier in an environment where they are neither demanded nor encouraged.

For the fortunate or gifted few who attain to positions of leadership in any form, the city offers freely both opportunity and stimulus which are rarely to be found in the country. It was perhaps these men in particular that William James had in mind when he wrote the following paragraph setting forth the effect of city conditions in speeding up a man's activities. The quotation is from an essay entitled "The Energies of Men," published in 1907:

As a rule men habitually use only a small part of the powers which they actually possess and which they might use under appropriate conditions. . . . We live subject to arrest by degrees of fatigue which we have come only from habit to obey. Most of us may learn to push the barrier farther off, and to live in perfect comfort on much higher levels of power.

Country people and city people, as a class, illustrate this difference. The rapid rate of life, the number of decisions in an hour, the many things to keep account of, in a busy city man's or woman's life, seem monstrous to a country brother. He doesn't see how we live at all. A day in New York or Chicago fills him with terror. The danger and noise make it appear like a permanent earthquake. But *settle* him there, and in a year or two he will have caught the pulse-beat. He will vibrate to the city's rhythms; and if he only succeeds in his avocation, whatever that may be, he will find joy in all the hurry and tension, he will keep pace as well as any of us, and get as much out of himself in any week as he ever did in ten weeks in the country.

There is nowhere in print a more eloquent statement of the possible expansion and development of a personality through being subjected to the demands of a highly organized urban environment. If even a minor fraction of the men and women who go forth from the farm to the city each year really do catch the pulse-beat and really do increase the effectiveness of their living even twofold or threefold—not to insist on Professor James's tenfold—this is one of the most important and significant consequences of the cityward drift of our population.

# THE MOVEMENT OF FARM POPULATION: ITS ECONOMIC CAUSES AND CONSEQUENCES

## BY ERNEST CHARLES YOUNG

The fraction of the total population that is engaged in agriculture has been decreasing since the time when reliable statistics first became available. This situation was initiated by the industrial revolution and the decrease has been more or less steady since that time. This fact is so much a commonplace as scarcely to need discussion, yet it is one of the most significant in our present economic problem.

Eighty-seven per cent of the persons gainfully employed in the United States in 1820 were engaged in agriculture. By 1840 this figure had decreased to 78 per cent, by 1900 to 35 per cent and by 1920 to 26 per cent. The census of 1930 will probably show about 20 per cent of those gainfully employed to be in agriculture.

This tendency is evident throughout the civilized world, but nowhere to the extent reported for the United States. In the last fifty years the ratio of agricultural population to total population has remained almost constant in France. In Germany the per cent of all persons gainfully employed who were engaged in agriculture dropped from 40 per cent in 1872 to 27 per cent in 1925. This is the greatest change reported for any important European country. In England only 10 per cent of those gainfully employed were engaged in agriculture as early as 1891.

This change is necessary to the progress of civilization. In 1820 only a very small fraction of the population was available to do other than provide food and clothing. In 1920, a small fraction of the population provided the food for all, and the great mass of the population was free to produce the many industrial products of modern life, to create the literature, develop the arts and sciences and to attend to the tremendous business of education which occupies so much of the life of the modern American.

Much of this change has been due to the increase in the efficiency of labor on the farm. The output per man in farming in the United States has increased steadily as is shown in Table I, until the output per man in 1927, as measured by grain production, was 102 per cent greater than that of 1870. Efficiency in farming as measured by physical production per worker was doubled during the fifty years from 1870 to 1920 according to estimates of the Bureau of Agricultural Economics.[1] During this period, efficiency in farming and in manufacturing has increased at about the same rate, but in railroading the rate of increase has been more rapid.

This apparent increase in efficiency is not all an actual gain to society. During this period many things that were formerly done on the farm have been transferred to the city. The manufacturing of farm machines and farm

[1] H. R. Tolley, *Proceedings of Land Grant College Association*, p. 243, February, 1927.

TABLE I

PRODUCTION PER PERSON ENGAGED IN AGRICULTURE IN THE
UNITED STATES 1870 TO 1927

| Year | Production of grain per person engaged in agriculture* (pounds) | Production of grain per person engaged in agriculture (per cent, 1870 = 100) |
|---|---|---|
| 1870 | 13,627 | 100 |
| 1880 | 16,971 | 125 |
| 1890 | 18,111 | 133 |
| 1900 | 18,459 | 135 |
| 1910 | 19,788 | 145 |
| 1920 | 24,162 | 177 |
| 1927 | 27,553† | 202 |

*Total production of corn, oats, wheat, barley, rye and buckwheat in the United States, as reported by the Bureau of Agricultural Economics. The figure for 1870 was found by adding the total production from 1866 to 1874 and dividing by 10, giving the average total production of grain. The total production was divided by the number of persons engaged in agriculture as reported by the census of occupations for that year.

†Production for 1927 is an average of the three years: 1926, 1927, and 1928. The number of persons engaged in agriculture in 1927 was estimated, from the number reported in 1920, by decreasing it in proportion to the decrease in farm population.

supplies in factories is essentially farm work. For purposes of the present discussion, however, this point is not important, as we are concerned with the output associated with each farmer rather than with his absolute efficiency.

While the output per man in agriculture and in industry has been increasing at about the same rate, there are important differences in the effects of these increases. The demand for most farm products taken individually or for all farm products taken collectively is relatively inelastic. The consumption of farm products in the United States is a function of population growth. Advertising may increase the consumption of a particular agricultural product but this is likely to be at the expense of other products. To the extent that farm products can serve as a source of raw material for new manufactured products other than food products the demand is subject to indefinite extension. The demand for most manufactured products taken individually or for all manufactured products taken collectively is elastic. Apparently the ability of the population to consume manufactured products is limited only by purchasing power.

As a result of this situation the effect of an increase in the output per man in farming is to make fewer persons necessary in the business because of the inelastic character of the demand. These persons set free (or rather forced out by competition) can find a place in the rapidly expanding manufacturing industry, the demand for whose products seems to be insatiable.

To the extent that farm products can find a market as a source of raw material for manufacturing products other than food products, it would appear that farming might enjoy this same expanding market. Agriculture seems to have lost rather than gained on this score. New manufacturing uses for vegetable oils, corn products, etc., have been developed, but the increased use of timber and mineral products has probably much more than offset this increase by substituting for farm produced raw materials in other manufacturing processes. The substitution of motor power for horse power in the United States has resulted in an increase in the amount of food available for human consumption. "The number of horses in this country declined about 750 thousand a year from 1921 to 1926. The hay and grain released if converted into meat would supply the meat requirements of our annual increase in population."[2] Farm products even when produced by the most efficient methods meet, with difficulty, the competition of virgin timber, coal and oil resources, the stored products of centuries of nature's efforts prior to man's development of agriculture.

Inasmuch as there are large areas in the world where people are underfed, it would seem that the development of foreign markets might furnish an outlet for increased agricultural output and thus avoid the necessity of drastic reduction in farm population. There are possibilities here, but the difficulty arises in the low purchasing power of these unexploited markets, which effectually prevents them from absorbing our farm products at prices at which we can produce them. The greater share of the population in these areas is engaged in agriculture. If these countries become industrialized they can absorb increased quantities of our food products.

In this situation the only alternative is decreased farm population, which viewed from the standpoint of society can scarcely be considered unfortunate. From the standpoint of the farmer, however, there has been much hardship. The agriculture of the civilized world has been under almost uninterrupted pressure since the beginning of the industrial revolution. Increasing efficiency in farming on the one hand has made competition keener on the farm and made fewer persons necessary; increas-

---

[2] L. J. Norton, "Some Recent Changes in Meat and Feed Crop Production," *Journal of Farm Economics*, Vol. IX, No. 3, July, 1927.

ing industrial output on the other hand has offered new opportunities in the manufacturing industries. Throughout this entire period farming must have been relatively less profitable, considering world agriculture, than other lines of activity; otherwise, we could not have had this long-term continuous shift in population. Population moves in the direction of economic opportunity. Sometimes these opportunities do not prove to be real or are only temporary. If population continues to move in a given direction for generations, it is conclusive evidence that a real difference in opportunity exists. During this time new agricultural areas have been opened and have offered new opportunities, and population has gravitated in that direction for a time. Although there have been temporary bright spots of this kind in the agricultural situation the continuous drift of population toward industry indicates that farming generally has been less attractive than industry. The older countries and the early developed agricultural communities in the United States have in general suffered the greatest population losses during this period. In these areas there has been a double population drain. Much of the drift to industry has been from such territory, and much of the movement of farm population to new farm territory has been from the same areas.

Another fact which tends to aggravate the farm population problem is the rapid natural increase in population in farm territory as compared to urban territory. A wife and children are economic assets on the farm but are often economic liabilities in the city. Marriage is at an earlier age, divorces are fewer, and families are larger in rural territory. Apparently, if left to themselves, and cut off from immigration, rural districts in America would increase in population about twice as fast as would cities.

While the farm population problem is one of long standing it has become particularly aggravated in recent years. Change in almost all lines of human activity is going on at an unprecedented rate. The industrial revolution is still in progress and gains momentum with the years. The present generation of farmers has probably witnessed greater changes in the technical aspects of production than any previous generation. Changes now taking place or imminent are likely to have as profound an influence as the development of the self binder. New ideas and new technical developments are adopted more quickly nowadays than formerly. This rapid progress of society is usually obtained at a cost. Frequently society obtains a tremendous advantage but the group may suffer.

Farm population changes as reported by the Bureau of Agricultural Economics are shown in Table II.

TABLE II

RATIO OF OTHER POPULATION TO FARM POPULATION*

| Year | Farm Population | Ratio of other population to farm population |
|------|----------------|-----------------------------------------------|
| 1910 | 32,076,960 | 1.9 |
| 1920 | 31,614,269 | 2.3 |
| 1925 | 28,981,668 | 3.0 |
| 1929 | 27,511,000 | 3.4 |

* Based on the census for census years and on estimates of the Bureau of Agricultural Economics for non-census years.

In 1910 there were 1.9 persons not on farms for each person living on a farm in the United States. In 1920 there were 2.3 persons and in 1929, 3.4 persons not on farms for each person on a farm.

The urbanization of our population has proceeded at a more rapid rate since 1920 than was ever reported before. This has been accomplished without any appreciable reduction in the production of farm products. This increase in output per man is due, in most part, to a change in the ratio of man power to the other factors in production rather than to an increase in the actual efficiency in the use of these other factors. There have been decreases in the material requirements for production but these have not been striking. In the last fifty years the introduction of new crop varieties, increased technical knowledge on the part of producers, and improvements in crops have probably not much more than balanced the losses due to increase in diseases and insects, the introduction of lower grades of land, and the exploitation of old lands. The index of crop yields has increased about ten per cent but much of this is the result of more intensive methods. It is not a measure of efficiency in the use of the factors of production. With livestock notable advances have been made in the rate of growth and the rate of production, but in part this has been a speeding up process rather than one of increasing efficiency in the use of feed and the other factors needed in production.

Considerable increase in output can be attributed to the better adjustment of production to environmental conditions through the selection of better adapted kinds and classes of crops and livestock. The tendency to market meat animals at younger ages and lighter weights than formerly is said to result in an increase in the efficiency in the use of feed. This is open to some question. Formerly there were large areas of cheap pasture and hay in the meat producing areas. Aged and slow growing animals can use a relatively large portion of their total feed in this form. Young and rapidly growing animals require more concentrated feed. They are adapted to conditions in which the ratio of concentrated feed to coarse rough feed and pasture is high. Dairy cows, hogs, and other animals using large quantities of concentrated feed have increased at the expense of the animals using principally coarse feed. When the total input is considered, these changes have probably resulted in little increase of efficiency. If the agricultural depression lasts long enough we will probably increase our hay and pasture and may return to less intensive methods of livestock production.

Some students of the agricultural problem expect the increased technical information in the hands of farmers, together with the effective agricultural educational machinery we have developed, so to increase the efficiency in the use of land and materials as to make the problem of the coming generation of farmers a more difficult one than the present.[3]

We have little evidence that increases of this kind are likely to bring about a revolutionary increase in agri-

---

[3] This point of view was well expressed in a paper by E. G. Nourse, "The Agricultural Outlook" presented at the meeting of the American Farm Economics Association, December, 1926, and published in the *Journal of Farm Economics*, Vol. IX, January, 1927.

cultural output. As the years go by, we have reported record yields of crops, and almost every year, the butter production record per cow is broken. This does not represent a corresponding increase in efficiency in the use of the factors of production. Most of these records simply represent new standards of intensity of production. The biological processes by which feed is converted into milk have not been greatly changed but we have learned how to increase the capacity of a cow for consuming milk making materials. These increases are subject to the law of diminishing returns and frequently are accompanied by decreased efficiency in the use of materials. O. E. Baker has shown that rather important increases in the rate of production of livestock and livestock products have taken place during the period since 1919.[4] Part of this increase may be due to the change from a generally unfavorable ratio of livestock prices to feed prices prior to 1920, to a very favorable one since that time.

G. F. Warren has shown that crop yields are a function of prices.[5] In discussing the outlook for agriculture in 1927 he said: "The effect of the agricultural depression is beginning to be apparent. The rapid increase in yields per acre has been checked, and apparently, a decline has begun. The effects become apparent very slowly because agriculture is a biological industry. At

---

[4] O. E. Baker, "Do We Need More Farm Land?" U. S. D. A. Mimeograph, 1928.

[5] G. F. Warren, "Crop Yields and Prices and Our Future Food Supply," *Cornell Agricultural Experiment Station Bulletin 341*, 1914. Also, discussion, "The Outlook for Agriculture," *Journal of Farm Economics*, January, 1927.

the present time, farmers are laying few tile drains. They are neglecting the upkeep of buildings and soils. Since the agricultural depression will probably last for a number of years, and since the full effects of the present methods are not apparent, I believe that crop yields will decline further. When the agricultural depression is over there will, I believe, be a period in which food will be expensive. The farmers of the United States know how to increase crop yields materially. They could probably increase the yields per acre by 25 per cent over present yields without great difficulty, provided prices were high enough, and provided they were allowed time enough in which to do it. There must be several years of prices that are high enough to restore confidence in agriculture before efforts to increase yields will begin. It will then require some time to check the decline before an increase will occur. When the agricultural depression is over it is probable that we will have twenty years in which much of the program of the American Economic Association will be devoted to some phase of the problems of the high cost of food."

The farm population question is so intimately associated with the problem of farm prosperity that one cannot be intelligently discussed without the other. The farm population problem will remain acute until farming again reaches a level of profit comparable to other lines of human activity. To date we have discovered no permanent cure for low prices and low profits in farming other than the movement of a part of the population out of farming into other activities. This is true whether the agricultural depression be due to unbalanced production of farm products or to the effects of deflation. Time does not permit more than this brief discussion of these two commonly accepted explanations of the depression.

While the movement of population out of farming is a sure cure for low prices and profits, it is not a quick cure. Farming because of its nature is a very slow business. It takes years of time and large quantities of materials and labor to build a farm business up into a going concern. Even the land itself absorbs large quantities of labor and material that become temporarily incorporated into it. A very considerable fraction of the land in a modern farm is capital. In periods of agricultural prosperity there is a tendency to build land up. Large quantities of labor and material are put into tile, fencing, buildings, soil improvement, and livestock improvement. This labor and material is in addition to that required in the normal production processes and adds to the total sum of the farm labor requirements. This capital investment serves as a reserve supply on which to draw in periods of agricultural distress. One of the features of the present agricultural depression has been the extent of capital depletion and the rate at which it has gone on. This is particularly true in marginal areas and on marginal land, where this capital feature of land may represent most of the land value.

Building operations have been at a standstill on farms for ten years. Painting, repair, and fence maintenance have been neglected. Drainage operations have been at a standstill. Fence rows remain uncut, land has been farmed harder and more carelessly. Breed improvement operations have almost ceased. Livestock quality and quantity have been depleted.

On thirty good farms in the best agricultural area in Indiana about half as much fence has been built per year since 1920 as was built per year during the previous ten year period. About ten per cent of the fence on these farms is now worthless and much more will become so, as the fence built from 1910 to 1920 becomes worn out. The situation on the average farm is undoubtedly much worse. This is the process by which capital is withdrawn from farming. It is a slow process. We have been at it ten years and the process is still continuing. On many farms this withdrawal of capital has proceeded about to the limit, as many a mortgage holder can testify who has recently acquired a farm of this type. The very rapid accumulation of farms in the hands of lenders in the last two or three years is a sign that these farms will become absorbers of materials and labor again or else operations must be discontinued. This withdrawal of capital makes possible a large temporary reduction in farm population.

In contrast to this situation of capital withdrawal in farming we have the reverse situation among urban industries and institutions. Probably never before in our history have urban capital investments increased with such rapidity. A large portion of the labor and materials absorbed in cities in the last ten years has gone into new capital—new buildings of all kinds, industrial, residential and public. Probably never before has urban property been in as good repair. It is conceivable that

within the next ten years we may reach a condition in
which urban property will be sufficiently built up and
rural property sufficiently run down to bring about
equilibrium or possibly a reversal of the process. In this
event, increased numbers of persons will be needed on
the farm. This population may be recruited from the
army that has been busy building new urban homes and
factories for the rapidly growing population to live and
work in.

Needless to say this process of alternately putting in
and taking out excessive quantities of capital is a very
inefficient one whether it be in the country or in the city.
The rapid increase in output per worker in farming is
evidently not all an increase in efficiency, but is partly
the result of neglect of repairs and improvements to
the physical plant in recent years.

Even under normal circumstances the reduction in
output would not be in proportion to the movement of
population. When economic pressure is put upon farming and a rapid movement of population out of the
industry is initiated, it is the marginal farmers and the
marginal workers that are most affected—those whose
"stake" in farming is small and whose output is meagre.
When times are hard, farmers and their families work
longer hours. Women and children do more field work.
To some extent the education of the children may suffer,
although most farmers are so convinced of the value of
education that they will endure real hardship themselves
rather than neglect it.

The deserted farmstead is one of the most noticeable
things in a country community that has been losing popu-

lation. The increased number of acres that can be cared
for per man is the principal cause in good agricultural
territory, but in the hilly sections of the eastern and
southern states, it is in most part the result of putting
land to less intensive use. Even in the corn belt a less
intensive use of land is evidenced by the increasing
areas of oats and grass. The cost of the improvements
on a farm have increased more rapidly in recent years
than have land values. In many areas the entire farm
will not sell for as much as the replacement cost of the
buildings. This has been true for many years in parts
of the Eastern United States but has recently become
so general that many farms on relatively good land
in Indiana and Ohio can be bought for less than the
replacement cost of the buildings.

Two forces have been at work to create this situation;
increasing building costs and decreasing population.
Undoubtedly most of the farm territory east of the
Mississippi River is over-built. There are more farmsteads than are needed and there is too much building
space per farm. In spite of this fact buildings are frequently inadequate because they have constituted such
poor investment that it has not always paid to modernize
them or even keep them in good repair. Changes in types
of farming, location of highways, and farm practice, as
well as new technical developments, cause buildings to
become obsolete.

Many industrial organizations follow the policy of
discarding old buildings and old equipment just as soon
as something better becomes available. Industrial property is generally much shorter lived than farm property.

The life of a good barn is fifty years or more. The uses to which a barn is put are such that it is likely to take many years to pay for it in use. Buildings constitute such a large portion of the total farm capital and pay for themselves so slowly that to discard them is out of the question.

Many farm units are preserved long after they would have been abandoned or merged with other units because a good set of farm improvements tempts a family to live on the farm and operate it as a unit. This is likely to result in the continuation of a more intensive type of farming than is warranted, it may hold back the introduction of new labor saving equipment, and it frequently results in poor utilization of labor and in excessive overhead.

Because the buildings in a community are being deserted and permitted to run down does not necessarily mean that agriculture is dying. It means that we must discard the old before we build the new. Just what type of agriculture, of farm organization, and of community life will develop when capital has been finally withdrawn from these obsolete improvements cannot be clearly foretold. In many areas a much less intensive type of farming will result. Probably we will have to try a lot of plans before the right one is found. Certainly no single plan will be generally adopted.

In the great plains region where settlement is recent and where improvements are relatively unimportant, adjustments have been going forward at a very rapid rate.

Professor W. E. Grimes in discussing this problem in the hard winter wheat belt says:[6]

The area per farm is increasing and will undoubtedly continue to increase. This movement is proceeding most rapidly in the newer sections where the resistance to changes in land tenure is less pronounced than in the older, more firmly established parts of the region.

The immediate effects of these changed conditions appear to be increased specialization in wheat production and the use of the combined harvester-thresher for custom work. Both of these moves may be but temporary expedients adopted to permit the handling of a larger wheat acreage per man and can be expected to disappear, to some degree at least, as the size of farms is slowly increased.

The sizes of combines and tractors now most commonly used in this region require farms of 1,000 to 4,000 acres to permit their most efficient utilization. This is two to four or five times as large an acreage as is included in the present usual farm of the area.

An increasing size of farms, if it materializes, will result in reduced farm population, and the number of people will be decreased. The extent of the effects of this movement may affect the number and the geographic limitations of political units within the region.

Many persons believe that we are about to witness changes away from the family type of farm organization into large operating units, or into small units operated in groups but subject to control by the general management.

---

[6] W. E. Grimes, "Farm Organization in the Hard Wheat Belt," *Journal of Farm Economics*, Vol. X, No. 2, p. 231, April, 1928.

The management problem on the farm becomes more acute each year.  Also the opportunities in management increase as farming becomes more complicated. The advantages of competent executive control of operations and financing and of division of labor become more evident as farming increases in complexity, but thus far, we have not learned how to take advantage of these forces to the extent to which they have been used in other industries. In some types of farming, particularly those followed in regions where a high degree of specialization is warranted, some progress has been made in this direction.  In the great diversified farming areas the family unit of operation seems likely to continue with perhaps some delegation of the management function to specialists employed cooperatively or by increase in the administrative function of the landlord or his agent.

The problem of carrying the burden of social institutions, churches, schools and hospitals in the country becomes more acute each year as the population diminishes.  The rapidly growing tendency in America to perform more service on a community basis aggravates the situation and adds to the burden.  The scope of this problem is such as to preclude its discussion here but it appears that a geographical reorganization of political units may be necessary, along with a change in the source from which taxes are collected and in the areas in which they are spent.

There is a commonly accepted notion that this heavy movement of population off the land is resulting in a difficult social problem. The assumption is that the best enter other occupations and the inferior individuals are left on the land. This theory would indicate development of a progressively inferior population group in the country. This idea is made still more tenable because a large proportion of our national leaders in non-agricultural lines were farm reared.

This contention is not substantiated by available data but rather the reverse is indicated. A large portion of the national leaders of the past generation came from the farm because a large percentage of our population was born in the country at that time. An examination of the present national leadership indicates that the origin of our national leadership is changing in about the same proportion as city births gain on rural births.

In New York about 30 per cent of the men who were born on the farm between 1850 and 1900 had left it. The rate, however, had changed from 25 per cent for those born in 1850 to 56 per cent for those born in 1890 to 1899. Sixty-two per cent of the men left the farm before they were twenty-five years of age. They left before they became deeply involved financially in farming.

After a farmer once becomes a farm operator he is not likely to leave the farm. In Livingston County, New York, of 447 farm owners in 1908 only seven per cent were in other occupations ten years later. Of 262 tenant farmers in the same area only 11 per cent had left farming in ten years. Many of these owners and tenants who had left the farm had entered less rigorous employment as a step towards retirement.

The general character of the occupations into which farm reared men go is indicated by a tabulation of the occupations of 757 men reared on farms in Jefferson and Tioga counties in New York. Out of this group there were only 12 professional men, six were merchants, the remainder other than farmers were wage earners. Although many of the nation's greatest men were farm reared, a large majority of those who leave the farm are in the ordinary positions of life. The city has a place for those of exceptional ability and for those with little ability. It is a place of extremes. A few leaders are needed but many followers. The agricultural depression has put a premium on efficiency and has increased the penalty for inefficiency.

"Income studies in central Indiana indicate a much wider variation in income than formerly existed. For the three years 1913-1915, the standard deviation in labor income in this region was $637 according to our studies, while for the three years 1925-1927, it was $1,248. For this latter period the variation in labor income was greater than for the extremely prosperous war year 1918, when the standard deviation in labor income was $1,135. During the three years 1925-1927, five per cent of these farmers made labor incomes in excess of $3,000; while during the extremely prosperous war period, 1916-1918, only seven per cent made labor incomes in excess of $3,000."[7]

[7] E. C. Young, "Economic Aspects of the Administration of Groups of Farms Under Northern Conditions," *Journal of Farm Economics*, Vol. XI, April, 1929.

The country demands efficiency. To gain a living in the country one must be self directed. Every farm needs at least one executive; even successful hired men must be largely self directed. The city can use large numbers of persons incapable of directing their own labor.

Space permits of only a few generalizations relative to the nature of farm population changes. These conclusions are based on studies in New York State reported in Cornell Experiment Station Bulletin 426.

1. Under economic pressure forcing a movement of population off the farm, persons are most likely to leave the farm in the following order:

  (a) Hired man
  (b) Farmer's son
  (c) Share tenant
  (d) Cash tenant
  (e) Owner operator

The more deeply a person becomes involved financially in agriculture, the less likely he is to leave the farm.

2. The attraction of other occupations for persons on farms varies directly as the difference in economic opportunity and inversely as the square of the distance to the opportunity.

3. Boys reared on large farms are more likely to stay on the farm than those reared on small farms.

4. Sons of hired men are more likely to leave the farm than sons of farm operators.

5. Older sons are more likely to leave the farm than younger sons.

6. Farmers with considerable property are less likely to leave the farm than farmers with little property.

7. Sons of farmers with considerable property are more likely to remain on the farms than sons of farmers having little property.

8. Within the farming community those who move about the least accumulate property most rapidly.

9. Farmers who come from other occupations or who leave the farm to return later do not accumulate wealth as rapidly as farmers who remain in the business.

The situation described in this paper seems like a dismal one but it should not be completely discouraging. We are paying the price of progress. Economic history since the beginning of the industrial revolution is a repetition of instances of groups of persons thrown out of employment by new machines. The small group may suffer for a time but even they are usually better off than their predecessors. Farming is a slow business; it responds slowly to economic forces but the response is sure.

# III

# FARM GROUP ACTIVITIES

# FARM GROUP ACTIVITIES IN THE SOUTH

## BY EUGENE CUNNINGHAM BRANSON

### PREFATORY REMARKS

Farm group activities is a phrase I use to mean the concert of farmers in economic, social and civic enterprises, either coöperative or corporative in character. The farmers of Denmark long ago discovered that group efforts were fundamentally necessary to success on every level of farm business, and equally necessary in the production, processing, financing, and distribution of farm volumes. Meantime the Danish farmers discovered that social and civic advantages were the certain fruits of organized comradeship. By 1850 their concerted group activities touched every phase of farm life, livelihood, and civic rule. They learned that, for most farm enterprises, coöperation was an effective form of business organization, but also that the corporation was a more effective business instrument for other farm businesses. Their land-mortgage credit societies are all corporations. Their abattoirs and margarine factories are frequently incorporated enterprises. They incorporate or coöperate according to the local situation or the character of the business. They have no fear of corporations. The substance of a thing is more important than the name of it, they say.

## I.   The Necessity for Farm Group Activities

The individual farmer standing alone is easily the victim of organized big businesses, not because big business is inherently wicked, but because unalert, unorganized farmers are merely mass details. Agriculture everywhere is dependent upon farm group activities and upon the cordial relationship of farm organizations with the local trade centers, with the country banks, the city banks, the national and international banks. The farmer's share of the consumer's dollar is directly and distinctly related to deft diplomacies, in dealings with trade, transportation, and credit organizations domestic and foreign. And it is my firm belief that Southern agriculture will rise in scale directly as it is properly related to the big world of business, and that the enduring victories lie in "collusion" rather than in collision. I use collusion, of course, in its original meaning of "playing the game together," not in its sinister common meaning. In the conflicting interests involved, both big business and the farmers can well afford to play the game together in generous, good-humored give-and-take. I profoundly believe in the enduring values of collusion in this sense.

1. Consider cotton. The ratio of the world's cotton supply produced in the South steadily decreases. The ratio of short staple cotton produced in the South steadily increases. Our short staple, less than an inch in length, is in competition with the short staple cottons of India, China, and Africa. The low production cost of short staple cotton in these far eastern countries

depresses the price level of our short staple in the markets of the world, and gradually lowers this price level until the Southern cotton planter finds himself with no profit left for his year's work. But there is another situation that threatens our cotton farmers east of the Mississippi. Unless we can produce cotton upon a low-cost basis equal to or lower than production costs in Texas, Arkansas, and Oklahoma, then the cotton farmers in the eastern cotton belt are doomed. In the annual cotton-growing contests conducted by *The Dallas News* during the last five or six years, the prize winners in Texas have produced cotton at from 3 to 6 cents a pound. Moreover, west of the Mississippi there is cotton acreage enough to produce America's full total of cotton for both domestic and foreign consumers.

Not impossibly the South Atlantic and the East South Central States are doomed to a dwindling, disappearing cotton agriculture. Not impossibly the story of cotton east of the Mississippi River in the future may be like the stories of indigo and rice culture in the long ago days of the South. Comparative advantage in low-cost cotton production lies west of the Mississippi, and it threatens beggary in our eastern cotton belt. The only way out lies in a rapidly increasing use of labor-saving, profit-producing machinery. That is to say, in mechanized farms tilled by owners, and only by farm-owner groups able and willing to buy and use tractors, gang plows, cultivators, harvesters, gins, and motor trucks on a community basis. We have so long produced cotton on a cropper-tenancy basis that most cotton farmers see no other way of cotton production. But already in a half-dozen states this method produces wide-spread poverty and bankruptcy, for tenants, landlords, supply-merchants and bankers alike. The only successful farming in the long run is farming by the men who own the land they till. Cropper-farming in the South is destructive of farm properties and at last it imperils human values, property values, tenants, landlords, merchants and bankers.

Fortunately, the Federal Farm Marketing Board is leading the way in organizing our farmers for group enterprises in behalf of adequate credit, adequate warehousing and orderly merchandising. The new outlook will appeal to alert farm owners. Our farm tenants cannot of course be organized for economic advantage. The farmers' profits or losses are the difference between production costs and price levels. And it is easier to control production costs than it is to control crop and livestock surpluses. Our cotton farmers' fate lies in low-cost production—in production costs so low as to be on the safe side of price levels. Price stabilization on high levels or on profit-producing levels is an exceedingly difficult problem, as the rubber and coffee producers have discovered. If nothing better than a reasonable price stabilization of cotton and tobacco results from the federal aid the farmers are now receiving, the achievement will be epoch-making. Whether or not organized effort can ever result in price-fixing is debatable. In any event the cotton and tobacco farmers of the South face the problem—the enormous problem—of producing these crops on a low-cost basis without lowering the standards of farm living. It can be done

in our Eastern cotton belt. Bruton and Thompson did
it on a Rockingham county farm in North Carolina in
1929. They produced lint cotton at three and a third
cents a pound, 1,677 pounds per acre. It was done by
intelligent farm owners with sufficient operative capital
under the expert guidance of our state college of agriculture. Such farmers need to be multiplied a hundred
thousand times over and distributed throughout our entire cotton belt. On page 203 of federal *Crops and
Markets*, June, 1929, issue, it appears that cotton production costs in 1928 ranged from seven cents to fifty-
two cents a pound. It is safe to say that the low-cost
cottons were produced by farm owners of the Bruton-
Thompson type, not by absentee landlords on a cropper-
farmer basis.

2. Our tobacco farmers face an even more difficult
problem, namely, the quality production of the tobaccos
that bring the highest prices. The volumes of these high-
grade tobaccos are now and have long been a small
ratio of the total tobacco crop. The low price of low-
grade tobaccos depresses the market prices offered for
all grades of tobacco leaf. Nothing short of effective
group action can increase the volume of high-grade
tobaccos properly graded and advantageously marketed. Here again federal farm aid invites the farmers'
participation, but the response will be in the main the
response of high-grade farmers, who produce their own
tobaccos on their own lands by their own labor or by
the competent direction of faithful overseers. The production of tobacco by undirected tenants and croppers
is fatal in the long run. Controlling the qualities and

quantities of tobacco leaf produced by absentee landlords is well-nigh a hopeless task.

3. It is proper to say, as Dr. James E. Boyle says,
that price levels are dominantly related to the volumes
of this or that farm commodity, but also it is proper
to say that another factor is related to the price levels of
cotton and tobacco, namely, their sale under controlled
circumstances. At present cotton and tobacco sales are
sales of distress commodities. The tenant must sur-
render these crops when his landlord calls for them.
They must be surrendered at the will of the supply-
merchants. The supply-merchants cannot hold them off
the market, for their own bills must be paid. The bulk
of both crops has passed out of the farmers' hands
by February 1 of every year. They must be dumped
upon the market and sold at distress prices, no matter
what the total volumes may be the country over. The
buyers have a chance to bid in these crops during the
first four marketing months at the prices they choose
to offer, or are directed to offer. In the ordinary tobacco warehouse the bids for the farmers' piles of
tobacco leaf suggest the prices offered in the bankruptcy sales of real estate or in the sheriff's sales of
property for taxes. I recently heard six fifteen-hundred-
dollar town lots bid off in a bankruptcy sale for fifty
dollars apiece. Relieving cotton and tobacco of forced
sale under distress conditions is a possibility with such
aid as the federal government is now organizing to
offer. But here again the cropper farmers are a menace
to the success of farm group enterprise. And clearly
the individual farmer can have no weight in determin-

ing what he receives for his tobacco. The problem is
difficult enough for organized farmers; it is utterly
impossible for solitary farmers.

4. In the United States for long years to come the
chances are that the bulk of farm commodities will be
produced on family-size farms. Spectacular accounts
of big-scale farms on a machine basis appear from time
to time in the periodicals of the country. Meantime the
census figures show a steady increase of medium-scale
and small-scale farms, and a steady decrease of big-
scale farms and large farms operated by owners
or their managers. Such enterprises as the Campbell
farm in Montana, the Taft farm in Texas, and the
Lowden farm at Sinissippi will continue to be rare.
So also the corporation cotton farm like that of the
Graniteville Mills in South Carolina. The fact is, farming is a business that does not easily submit to big-
scale business methods. There will be successes here
and there, but they will be few. The more immediate
problem is the motorizing and mechanizing of family-
size farms. The average size of farms in Denmark and
in North Carolina is only twenty-six cultivated acres.
But the farmers in Denmark are machine farmers in
the main, while in North Carolina they are mainly
hand-power, mule-power farmers. The Danish farmers
lower production costs by the group ownership and
operation of the expensive machines they need—tractors, gang plows, motor trucks, seeding machines, har-
vesting machines and the like. In this way they have
reduced to a minimum the huge cost of human and
workstock labor. Group organization of this sort in

Denmark extends even to waterworks, light, heat, power, and telephone services in country communities. True the farm regions of Denmark are densely populated, being 216 per square mile, against 42 per square mile in North Carolina. The sparsity of rural population in the South of course makes community group effort difficult.

My opinion is that reducing farm production costs lies in the more or less rapid mechanizing of medium-scale and small-scale farms, rather than in the direction of big-scale farms on a corporation basis.

Somehow or other this lowering of farm production costs must rapidly develop on Southern farms. It is a matter of sheer survival for the farmers of the South to keep on the safe side of the deadline of profits, and their only chance lies in producing crops at the lowest possible cost-unit. The ideal is the largest possible volumes of the highest possible values at the lowest possible cost-unit of production. And this problem must be solved on the small-scale farms of the South or we shall have a disappearing agriculture in our cotton and tobacco areas. It goes without saying that the only possible way of lowering production cost lies in the reënforcing of human labor by horse and machine power—a most difficult problem in tobacco production because tobacco is essentially a handmade crop. Here the readiest way out lies in the low-cost production of high-grade tobaccos, and this result depends directly upon the expert guidance and unremitting supervision of competent landlords and overseers.

## II. Obstacles

It is impossible in a brief address to do more than itemize the obstacles in the way of farm group activities in the South. They have been treated at length in the weekly issues of the North Carolina University *News Letter* and in the North Carolina Club Year-Books during the last sixteen years. Very largely these obstacles are social conditions but in every instance they produce economic consequences that lower the levels of life for the vast majority of farm workers in the South. In brief these obstacles are:

1. Sparsity of farm population—meaning too few farm families to the square mile, and these few settled not in country communities, but in solitary farmsteads scattered throughout the vast open spaces of the South. The average in North Carolina is seven farm families per square mile; it is only one farm family per square mile in eleven Texas counties. We have country neighborhoods and settlements. We have few farm communities in any Southern state. It is a situation that makes farm community efforts difficult or impossible. Remote from improved highways, many farm areas are static or even stagnant. There is a "dark corner" in almost every Southern county.

 · 2. Sheer-illiteracy and near-illiteracy are excessive in the farm regions of the South. In Denmark the illiterates are only two per thousand; in North Carolina they are one-hundred ninety per thousand in the rural regions alone. The census figures give us approximately

the volumes of sheer illiteracy, that is to say, the illiteracy of self-confessed illiterates. Right around ninety
per cent of the native white illiteracy of every Southern
State is found in the rural regions. Our towns and
cities have reduced their illiteracy ratios to a minimum.
The problem of illiteracy in the South is mainly a
country problem both for whites and blacks. Near-
illiterates are the vast numbers of people who can read
a little but who do not read at all, who can think, perhaps, but who do not or will not think. Every social
worker knows how difficult it is to help people who
do not read and who cannot or will not think. Jacking
up the levels of Southern agriculture means in large
part the rapid elimination of illiteracy in all its forms
among whites and blacks alike in our farm regions.
Approximately one-third of all the native-born white
illiterates of the Nation are in the South and mainly in
the rural South. Near-illiteracy is an indictment that
Mr. Vanderlip laid upon the whole United States. We
are a Nation of economic illiterates, said he. Economic
illiteracy is but one of the varieties of illiteracy. There
are others.

3. Excessive farm tenancy, mainly of the cropper
type, is another serious social ill in the Southern States,
and just here it is well to say that farm tenancy in the
South is an expression of poverty. In the case of the crop-
per-farmer it means unmitigated poverty. Elsewhere
in the United States farm tenancy is largely an economic problem. In the Middle and Far West farm
tenancy is a phase of capitalism. In these areas farm
tenants are frequently cash renters. Even oftener they

are tenants who are able to pay rents in cash. They think it is good sense and good business to cultivate other people's farms on shares, and to use their capital for operative purposes. There is hardly a trace of such tenancy anywhere in the South. More than half of all the farmers of the South, both races counted, are tenants and more than half of our tenants are croppers and share tenants. Here again is an obstacle that stands squarely across the way of farm group organization and activities either economic, social or civic. We know that areas of excessive farm tenancy in the South are areas of excessive illiteracy, that farm tenancy produces country illiteracy and that country illiteracy in turn produces farm tenancy, that farm tenancy and country illiteracy are twin-born social ills and that neither can be cured without curing the other.

4. Ill-balanced diets in our rural regions produce deficiency diseases—pellagra in particular. Pellagra threatens to produce excessive ratios of insanity and mortality in our rural regions and mill villages. Tuberculosis in our country regions is rising into alarming proportions, and it is hard to reach and treat it successfully under rural conditions. Hookworm has not yet been appreciably decreased. Malaria is still a fundamental problem in the Southern States. Here and there gigantic effort has been followed by almost miraculous results. There is no more of it in Georgia than in other Southern States but recent surveys in that State show alarming malarial conditions. Rural health conditions in general in the South are crippling and disabling to a civilization three-fourths of which is rural.

Alabama and North Carolina are leading the South in county health units but the vast majority of Southern counties have no public health organizations. Public health workers face great difficulty in reaching and serving rural homes in the South. All these obstacles are directly related to effective farm group activities.

5. Town-Country Antagonisms—here is a fundamental matter related to an improved agriculture. There are very few towns in the South as yet that give any generous thought to the farmers within their trade territories. It is hard to bring our towns and cities to a realization that it is impossible for towns and cities to grow fat in a lean countryside. Without the active help of our towns and cities the farmers are not likely to solve any of their problems.

Los Angeles is perhaps doing more for the farmers of Southern California than any other city in the United States is doing for the farmers in its trade area. It is distinctly a country-minded city. The Marketing Exchanges of the farmers of Southern California are in Los Angeles. Rural Social-Economics is a subject taught in all the country schools of the county but also in the city schools of Los Angeles. Acquaintance with rural social-economics is required of all public school teachers, town and country. The city schools of Los Angeles offer to city pupils courses in rural sociology and rural economics. Most people know Los Angeles as a great motion picture center. But as a matter of fact it is a great country life center—the most effective in the United States.

### III. THE SOCIAL AND ECONOMIC LAG

Improved roads, motor trucks, motor cars, country telephones and radios are agencies of socialization. Gradually the farmers of the South will capitalize our public highways. I see signs of it everywhere. They are comforting signs but the responses are relatively few as yet. Never in any other country of the world have the farmers ever had such a chance as they now have in America to capitalize transportation and communication facilities. It is now possible for them to rise out of domestic into commercial levels of food, feed, and livestock farming, and in the South to end their servitude to cotton and tobacco as money crops. Nearly anything our farmers can produce can now find its way into the homes of consumers far and near. I have on my desk a long list of farmers who are now making more money than they ever made before in all their lives. They are supplementing their cotton-tobacco incomes by producing and selling home-cured hams, sausages, eggs, poultry, whole milk, fruits and vegetables of every sort. And they are rapidly learning to process and package these products properly. The improved facilities of transportation and communication are a way of escape for our cotton and tobacco farmers when these standard crops fail them as a source of money income.

The social and economic lag of our country population in the South is excessive. The social agencies of America have found it extremely difficult or impossible to get into the rural South. The moneys and the efforts of the great foundations for child welfare, recreation, sanitation and hygiene, and other similar social aims have gone in the main to city dwellers. Just why these organizations fail to reach rural people is set forth on a fact foundation in a recent volume on *How Shall Country Youth Be Served?* by Harlan Douglass.

Whatever else appears in the Country Life section of the Virginia Institute of Public Affairs, it seems to me to be clear that the country life of the Nation is worth saving, that it is a gigantic task, that in the main it is the task of the farmers themselves, that unorganizable farmers imperil both farm life and national life in all its manifold phases, and above all, that the way out for a stricken farm population lies in organized farm group activities inspired by the conviction that comradeship is more effective and enduring than fierce contests of the beak-and-talon, tooth-and-claw type. We must learn like the Danish farmers that class organization for class advantages alone is a doubtful basis for group activities.

# THE EASTERN SHORE OF VIRGINIA PRODUCE EXCHANGE

## BY BENJAMIN T. GUNTER

I have been asked to talk on "Farm Group Activities," and in connection therewith relate my experiences with the Eastern Shore of Virginia Produce Exchange.

The Eastern Shore of Virginia Produce Exchange was organized before the days of "coöperative marketing" organizations, at a time when the word "coöperative" had not been overworked. At that time (1900), when the charter for this organization was secured and the by-laws to control its operations were adopted, there was no similar organization in this country, or certainly in the East; no star or chart to which the Committee of twelve, to whom was intrusted the task of drafting a plan of organization which we were hoping would relieve us in our distress, could look for guidance. Not a member of our Committee had had any experience in marketing. With main strength and awkwardness we essayed the task, and it is, indeed, remarkable that out of our labors came a plan which has been wonderfully successful and so acceptable that it has in thirty years of active operation needed but few changes to make it meet the requirements of a successful coöperative marketing organization.

My only experience in the marketing problem has been with a coöperative marketing organization, so I shall confine myself entirely to this particular group activity.

Congress has undertaken to provide for associations of this character. "An Act to authorize associations of producers of agricultural products," known as the Capper-Volstead Act, provides:

That persons engaged in the production of agricultural products, as farmers, planters, ranchmen, dairymen, nut or fruit growers may act together in Associations, corporate or otherwise, with or without capital stock, in collectively processing, preparing for market, handling and marketing in interstate or foreign commerce, such products of persons so engaged. Such associations may have marketing agencies in common; and such associations and their members may make the necessary contracts and agreements to effect such purposes; Provided, however, That such Associations are operated for the mutual benefit of the members thereof, as such producers, and conform to one or both of the following requirements:

First: That no member of the association is allowed more than one vote because of the amount of stock or membership capital he may own therein; or

Second: That the association does not pay dividends on stock or membership capital in excess of eight per centum per annum.

And in any case to the following:

Third: That the association shall not deal in the products of non-members to an amount greater in value than such as are handled by it for members.

"Coöperative" farmers' associations are looked upon with favor both by Federal and State authorities. Those organizations of farmers that are regarded by the government as coöperative are not so likely to be considered as violating trust laws and operating in restraint of trade as will other associations not so organized.

We know by experience that it is helpful, when under investigation, to be looked upon with favor.

So, then, farmers may organize under the Capper-Volstead Act, and if their charter allows only one vote for each member, regardless of stock owned by him, or limits its dividends to eight per cent on capital stock, and provides further that the association does not market more produce for non-members than it does for members, such a concern will be regarded as a "co-operative organization."

The Eastern Shore of Virginia Produce Exchange was chartered by the General Assembly of Virginia in an act approved January 26, 1900, and in this act it was stated that,

The general objects and purposes of said corporation shall be the buying and selling of produce as agent of the producer, the consigning of produce as agent of the producer, inspecting all produce it may handle, owning and operating storage warehouses and packing houses for produce, and generally all other lawful things customarily connected with the trade known as the produce business.

The capital stock of the company was to be not less than $5,000.00 nor more than $50,000.00. The membership was to be composed of three classes:

First: Stockholders. These own stock and enjoy all privileges.

Second: Tenants of stockholders. These live on lands of stockholders and have the right to market their produce through the organization.

Third: Shipping privilege members. One dollar will purchase a shipping privilege. Many negroes own shipping privilege certificates. These certificates entitle the holders to all rights of membership, including participation in the patronage dividend, except the right to vote in general or local division meetings.

The association confines its operations almost exclusively to marketing highly perishable crops, cabbage, strawberries, Irish and sweet potatoes, grown in the two counties of the Eastern Shore of Virginia, Accomac and Northampton. It has a local division at each shipping point, 48 in all, and each local division elects a director, making in all 44 directors. It has a Department of Standards and Measures, and one or more inspectors for each division. All inspectors are nominated by the Manager of the Department of Standards and Measures, and elected by the Board of Directors.

## REASONS FOR THE ORGANIZATION

The organization was born of despair. For several years farming operations had been conducted at a loss. Young men were leaving farms. Landowners were moving from farms to villages. Produce was frequently left in the ground because the price of the commodity would not justify its being marketed. At that time only about six markets were open to us. Distribution generally was out of the question. All marketing conditions were chaotic. Postage stamps were sometimes used in payment for produce shipped, so small was the return.

A careful study of the situation convinced the Committee of twelve, charged with the duty of recommending some plan for the bettering of marketing conditions, that a number of changes must be made in our methods of marketing. Some of those changes, at the present time accepted as commonplace, were at that time new and radical. Some of these may be briefly enumerated as follows: A wide distribution of all our produce in all possible markets, thereby preventing an oversupply in any one market, with its consequent demoralization; prevention of ruinous competition on the part of dealers at home who were selling or consigning all produce at a certain sum per package, regardless of price; intelligent salesmanship upon the part of an agent of the farmer, employed at a stipulated salary, whose duty it would be to market for the farmer at the best price obtainable; daily communication with all the markets of this country, as well as Canada and Cuba, by telegraph and telephone; the building of a reputation for honesty and fair dealing with the trade, thereby expecting to command for all produce a preference, if not a premium; to take care of the small producer as well as the large producer, furnishing to each the same and ample facilities for marketing his produce; to sell all produce as far as possible f.o.b. loading points. However commonplace these changes in our methods of marketing may seem today, they were at that time regarded as questionable, not practical,—the theories of dreamers. It was a task of no small proportions to undertake to educate our farmers up to the realization of the possible aid that might be rendered by these suggestions. Prejudices had to be overcome. Ignorance and suspicion on the part of many had to be dealt with.

To undertake the task, it was necessary to have capital. The shares were placed at $5.00 each. Those financially able to subscribe were doubtful and evasive. Others were willing to subscribe, but they did not have the money. We accepted as low as twenty-five cents per share, the remainder of the $5.00 to be paid at crop time. At no time was the maximum of $50,000.00 stock issued. Zealous stockholders borrowed money for the necessary funds with which to conduct the business. Our faith was strong. This had much to do with saving the day.

The first real test came when we said to the farmer: "You expect the trade to be honest with you, and you must be honest with the trade. You must give the purchaser a good merchantable product, packed in a fair sized and sightly package." At that time there was no legal standard package or barrel. Large barrels and small barrels were used.

### Standardization

All of the above led inevitably to standardization of all produce received for sale. Such drastic measures as inspection of all goods at time of loading and proper classification of same had never been undertaken by anyone, at least, in this section of the country. The association adopted a brand known as the "Red Star," and the trade was given to understand and know that "Red Star" potatoes when sold as such must measure up to a certain size potato. In order to accomplish this, it was absolutely necessary to adopt a system of inspection that would insure proper grading. Neither money nor time was spared in accomplishing this result. Hundreds of thousands of dollars, a million will not cover the entire amount, have been spent by the organization in building up the reputation of the "Red Star." It is known and recognized for its superior quality in all the markets of this country and in Canada and Cuba. This policy enabled all produce, or practically all produce of members, to be sold f.o.b. loading point. This was an innovation in marketing, and a very desirable one.

To bring about these results it was necessary to educate the farmer. It soon became necessary for every marketing agency to establish a brand and adopt some system of inspection more or less rigid.

Investigation and study from time to time by the United States Department of Agriculture convinced us not only that the system was feasible, but that it was necessary. The Department gave careful consideration to the matter, and its agents spent some time investigating our methods and our grades and adopted and promulgated two grades known as U. S. Grade No. 1 and U. S. Grade No. 2, these grades corresponding to the "Red Star" grade and the "Gear Wheel" grade, the first and second grades of our organization. And to aid in carrying out such a system, the United States Department of Agriculture, in conjunction with the State, employs inspectors whose services can be secured by anyone desiring them. Their system, unlike ours, does not grade. It tells the owner of the car if the produce in the given car inspected measures up to U. S. Grade No. 1 or No. 2, as the case may be. The

owner, if he so desires, ships or sells it regardless of
the report of the inspector.

## SOME ESSENTIALS TO SUCCESSFUL OPERATION

1. *Capital.*—A working fund sufficiently large to
care for the purchase of equipment of every descrip-
tion, supplies, and salaries of officers and employees,
including a large number of inspectors, most of whom
are paid definite salaries and without commission, is
necessary. Farmers as a rule, particularly tenants, can
not wait until their produce has reached the markets
and returns therefor made to the organization in the
ordinary and usual course of trade. This, under the
most approved methods, would consume too much time.
The delay is too great. It frequently requires ten to
twelve days to complete delivery. This money may
come from the sale of capital stock. It is true at first no
corporation with capital was regarded as truly co-
operative. To be truly coöperative such organizations
must be non-stock corporations. Many such organizations failed for lack of capital. Then it was realized
that capital was absolutely essential and it was regarded
as legitimate to have capital, but the dividends should
be limited, and stock widely distributed with as few
shares as possible to any one person. The only change
made by the Eastern Shore of Virginia Produce Exchange to conform to the approved definition of a co-
operative association was to provide through by-law
that there should be no dividend on capital stock in
excess of eight per cent, in the place of ten per cent as
theretofore paid. After having created a surplus fund

of approximately $200,000.00, it was further provided that all net earnings, after paying eight per cent dividend on stock, should be divided into two parts, one carried to the surplus fund, and the other returned to the grower in the proportion in which he had contributed to the entire fund. So well have the business methods of the Eastern Shore of Virginia Produce Exchange been recognized by bankers, that it has not suffered for credit. Its borrowings for a short period each year during the operating season exceed a million dollars.

2. *Volume of Business Controlled.*—It is absolutely essential that the organization have control of as large a volume of the commodity to be marketed as possible. Perhaps it is never possible to secure the entire crop grown, but the larger the percentage controlled the more efficient will be the operations and the greater the return to the members. How to secure control of the largest volume of the marketable commodity has been one of the most difficult problems to be solved. When our organization undertook to solve this problem, it did not consider the contract theory. It was necessary, without contract, to fetter the farmer, for thus he regarded all limitations and restrictions, without binding him by written contract to market all produce grown by him through the organization. He was, without contract, to be transformed overnight, from a free lance in marketing, to an efficient packer. We concluded that to hold him we must show him a profit over and above his neighbor, who continued to market in the good old way his father had marketed. In other words, we ex-

pected to hold him by results. The wisdom of this policy we think has been demonstrated. If we can not benefit him, there is no justification in holding him. He should be free. Loyalty that comes from the binding force of a contract, without results to justify it, will not sustain the organization. Perhaps a great majority of coöperative organizations rely upon the contract system.

3. *Standardization.*—Standardization and grading and branding of all produce are essential to success. The importance of these can not be overestimated. These measures beget confidence with the trade. It costs a great deal, but it pays. Perhaps enough has been said of the necessity of grading and branding to make it unnecessary to deal further with it here.

4. *Pooling Prices.*—Prices for perishable commodities not infrequently change during the day. Prices are not the same on all markets on a given day. Sometimes the supply on a given day exceeds the demand, and part of the supply must be carried over, though loaded and ready for shipment, to another day when the price will be lower. What then must be done? Pooling under the circumstances seems to be the only fair way. Our practice then is to give to every patron, whose produce is received, graded, loaded and ready for market on a given day, the same price for the same grade. It was early discovered that no other practice would be just or satisfactory; hence, the practice adopted by us known as "pooling prices."

5. *Proper Audits of All Accounts.*—Perhaps no one feature will insure as much confidence on the part of

all patrons as a careful audit of all accounts. The Eastern Shore of Virginia Produce Exchange at the close of each marketing year, just prior to the annual stockholders' meeting, has all books and accounts at the General Office audited by a certified public accountant. Though the volume of business each year runs up into the millions of dollars, and the duties of the accounting department are very exacting, no accountant, so far as I recall, during the entire time, certainly in the last twenty-five years, has ever detected an error of a penny. The books of all local agents who receive from the Central, or General Office the returns of the individual shipper and disburse the same, are each year audited by the bookkeeping department of the General Office. Sometimes errors are detected, due to many things, but these errors are corrected and the shipper is thus insured that he has received every penny to which he is entitled for his produce. This one feature makes the landlord encourage his tenant to ship through the organization. In every settlement with the farmer the account of sales shows gross sales and all deductions.

6. *Management.*—You may have capital; you may have volume of business; you may have standardization; you may pool prices; you may have the best business methods; still, to be successful and grow, you must have intelligent and efficient management. Without this, any organization, however coöperative it may be, will soon pass out of existence. Your sales force must be alert and competent. Their task is a hard one. It calls for something more than a high order of intelligence. It demands real capacity to deal with all sorts of

characters, honest and otherwise, and sell them your product. Then, too, while the sales are being made, the distribution wide, the treasurer must not be overlooked. His task is a hard one. To use a homely expression, "The salesmen feed the cow, while the treasurer does the milking." You may feed, but you must have a good milker.

I have touched only the high spots in considering the essentials for a successful coöperative marketing organization or association. Its possibilities are great, but its difficulties are many. Its foes are many. For generations untold the farmer has been exploited. He has toiled long and incessantly. A sprightly young neighbor, of a covetous nature, not willing to toil, sets himself up as a marketer. He solicits his neighbor's produce. The neighbor, not so intelligent it may be, listens to his mellifluous words and propaganda, and turns over his produce to his would-be friend. The farmer's interest is not considered. His prejudices are appealed to. He is told what a big salary the manager is getting, or it may be the treasurer, or some one else, and he feels outraged and responds liberally with his produce to his supposed friend. He finds out his mistake too late. The poison has been inserted. He disliked the coöperative association. He blames all of his ills on it. Not logical, we must admit, but nevertheless true. Again the farmer does not like to be controlled. He frets when told that his produce must measure up to a certain standard; that he must not harvest on a certain day. He has been accustomed to doing as he pleases. He is being deprived of his liberties. So the organization is beset with foes from within as well as without. Then, too, all of these foes, when there is a crop failure or overproduction of the particular crop harvested, and the net return to the farmer meager, combine and with all sorts of propaganda, some half-true and unexplained, exceedingly dangerous, and some entirely false, make a determined assault on the coöperative association. On one occasion a desperate attempt was made on the Eastern Shore of Virginia Produce Exchange. Some who wished to become officers in the organization, some would-be politicians aspiring to preferment, saw an excellent opportunity to make a drive against this particular organization. Their mightiest assault was made on the stock feature. They clamored for one vote, no matter how many shares the owner held. Friends became embittered. The attack failed in accomplishing its purpose, though for a few years the organization was weakened. The defeated assaulters went forth and organized a new association with one vote, no matter how many shares held. It was an "Exchange," and to all intents and purposes an ideal organization. Its members endorsed notes to the extent of $60,000.00, and paid them out of their own pockets, and besides some got nothing for their produce, while others were only paid in part.

Despite the comments and assaults above referred to, there is still another class who damn it with faint praise,—"It is not perfect but it is the best we have got." They admit they want their tenants to use the organization, because they say they know it represents an honest return to them and insures their rent.

The Eastern Shore of Virginia Produce Exchange, it is true, was a pioneer in marketing as a coöperative association and lacked experience along this line, yet it has been wonderfully successful. The first year of its existence its total volume amounted to $750,000.00. From this comparatively small beginning, it grew annually until it reached its peak in 1920 when its volume amounted to $20,000,000.00. This was an unusual year, when prices for all produce were phenomenal. It has for the last few years marketed about 70 per cent of the entire output of the two counties. In dollars the business in the last few years has totaled from $6,000,000.00 to $7,000,000.00 annually.

# IV

# THE FARM FAMILY

# THE FARM FAMILY:

## ITS CONTRIBUTION TO THE NATION

### BY FLORENCE ELIZABETH WARD

The family was our first and continues to be our most important institution—taking precedence over the church and the school in its significance as a training ground for life.

Farming is the only occupation in which the family operates as an occupational unit. Thus it may be said that agriculture—the nation's primary industry, involving its largest capital and the greatest number of its workers,—is made up of six millions of family partnerships with individual units dotting the mountain sides, valleys and plains of the forty-eight states, where every pair of hands, even small hands, and every pair of feet, are having some part in contributing to the nation's welfare, in the production and distribution of its food.

"Man may not live by bread alone"—but he must have bread. The economic contribution of agriculture needs neither elucidation nor proof here. We all know that the wealth of our cities is the result of agriculture, that the city dweller is absolutely dependent on the farmer for his "bread"—be it wheat or meat, fruit or vegetables. We understand, too, that in the future the contribution of agriculture will depend upon the earning power of the land, not upon its appreciation in value.

It is of these things in our national well-being, over and above "bread alone" contributed by the farm family, that I wish to speak.

The producing of food from nature's storehouse on 924,000,000 acres is a material contribution without which our nation would perish. The producing of citizens on six millions of farm homesteads is an inestimable human contribution without which our nation would suffer deeply because of those intangible, but important, benefits that have their origin in the very special characteristics of those who live close to the soil. I am thinking of the quality of the boys and girls who leave the farm for the city—of their sturdiness, resourcefulness, intelligence and physical vigor. I see behind this younger group the fathers and mothers who have trained and guided them and sent them forth, themselves remaining to wrestle with the production of that "bread" of which we all have need. I want to point out some of the handicaps under which these farm mothers and fathers labor—I want to emphasize the importance of assuring to these rural families and their children an adequate share of the satisfactions of life, because of the importance of their contribution to the nation. Finally, I want to suggest the agencies through which some of their difficulties are being and will be removed, so that an increasingly rich and far flung contribution to the nation may be made.

## The Farm Family of Today

The development of this country during the last 100 years has been from a rural to an urban population, which fact shows that the farm family's contribution to the nation has been one of human beings. The farm has provided the influx of fresh young blood to the cities—the boys and girls who have grown up in the country and who because of ambition, a spirit of adventure, a longing for a wider horizon, or a feeling that they were no longer needed at home, have come to the towns and participated in the work they found there. The cities need these young men and women from the rural districts and it is entirely normal that a certain percentage of them should arrive each year—vigorous, wholesome, mentally alert offspring of hardworking, sturdy parents. Because of the situation in immigration at the present time this continuous contribution of human material from the farm family is of increased importance.

Modern farming is not a matter of brawn alone. Manual labor plays a smaller part than formerly and good management, marketing skill, and a knowledge of machinery, are determining factors in success. Scientific agriculture has superseded traditional practices, and the present day farmer, to make good, must have business and managerial ability. He must deal with intricate problems of the disposal of his product, he must know how to control insect pests and plant diseases. He must understand how to nurture his soil if he would make it yield adequately and provide a living for himself and his family.

This intelligent new farmer has new standards of living, he makes new demands on life. His condition should not be compared with the farmer of 25 or 50 years ago, but with that of the man living in the city, with equivalent intelligence and thrift. Does he have more or less comfort in his home? Does his wife work harder or has she household equipment as satisfactory as that of her city sister? Do his children have equal opportunity with city children in respect to culture and happiness—education, recreation, physical care? The living standards held by the modern farm family are the "motivating force" which determines eventually whether or not they will remain on the farm. Will it prove the best place in which to satisfy their longings for the "good life" or will they migrate to the city to seek wider opportunities for their children; greater comfort, leisure and variety of living? Viewed from the purely selfish angle it is obviously the business of the nation to see that the producers of its "bread" have all possible incentive to continue the pursuit of agriculture.

To offset the apparent selfishness of this aim, it should be said that for the most part, rural people love the country and prefer to remain there, provided they can at at the same time satisfy their ambitions for their children and their standards of comfort for themselves.

The marginal farmer—the heavy, unimaginative, phlegmatic type who is content to plod along in the ways of his father before him, has no place in the future scheme of agriculture which must be efficient from the economic standpoint. His elimination is one of the problems of today. He cannot compete with the up-to-date successfully managed farm, and his place is wherever there is a keener mind to direct him, either hired by another farmer or working in a routine city job. It is with the other type of farmer and farm family that we are at present concerned.

## FARM AND FARM HOME INSEPARABLE

The business of farming differs from all other occupations because the home and the business plant are so closely linked and so necessary to each other. This fact makes the farm woman of greater importance to the economic success of her husband than the homemaker is in the case of any other type of business man. Whereas the activities of the farm household constantly dovetail into and supplement those of the farm routine, the home of the banker, the grocer, the lawyer or any other commercial or professional man is to a large extent a liability—something that involves expense without augmenting his profits. The farm home is also the headquarters for the farm business office; the by-products of the farm business furnish food, fuel and other benefits to the farm family, for which the city man must earn cash; the atmosphere of the farm home—its orderliness, its serenity, its efficiency or lack of it, have an immediate effect on the farmer, because he is constantly in contact with it; the members of the farm household constitute a corps of trained workers, each expected from earliest childhood to bear a share of the necessary work that results in the benefits enjoyed by all. The pull of the city on the younger members of a family is *out*. They go out for companionship, amusement, social life. The pull of the farm home is *in*. Their desires are satisfied within the family circle.

This coherence of the farm family is one of its most important characteristics. It has a marked bearing on the quality of the human material—the boys and girls from farm families—who leave their rural homes for one reason or another to take up life in other places. The habit of work, and the habit of working together for a common good has become ingrained in these young people. Their independence and self-reliance is attested by the very fact of their leaving the home shelter. Many of them have had training in leadership in the club work of which I shall speak shortly. They have learned to be thrifty with what they have because they have had to make the most of so little. They distinguish between the solid and real, and the superficial and artificial. Theirs is a sturdiness of character and a singleness of moral standard engendered by the simple piety of their home surroundings. They have a love of beauty and spaciousness because they have always lived within sight of the beauty of stretching fields and distant hills.

Children who have gained all these qualities from their home surroundings have a deep-seated love for their home and those in it. They may go away for a time, but they return as often as they can. They bring back the leaven of new ideas, and the inspiration gained by seeing how other people live and what they enjoy. They want the best for their own families and if there is no way in which the best can be carried to the farm they are likely to try persuading the farm family to migrate. Hence it behooves us to encourage those agencies which enrich farm life.

## THE FARM WOMAN

The guiding hand in the growth of these forward-moving young people in the farm home, is, of course, the mother. The prediction from those who are in a position to know is that the farm woman is coming to be more and more a unique and outstanding figure among women in any walk of life. She is, in a way, the center of interest in the farm home, for it is her task to gather all its component threads together and weave them into a strong and consistent pattern. She is so much more than just a housekeeper, although, like all homemakers, her time is largely occupied with the preparation of meals, keeping the house and the linen clean, sewing, and caring for the small children. These are the visible activities of her household life. Throughout all of them she is, whether she recognizes it or not, creating an atmosphere, setting up her standards, teaching her methods. Necessity demands that in order to get the work of the household done she must require as high a level of accomplishment from her family. While she and her husband may have talked over together their ambitions and plans for their children, it is usually the mother's business to see that these are carried out.

. More than this: The farm mother is often her husband's partner in production. She may not often actually till the fields, as the European peasant women do, but she frequently milks the cows, makes butter

and almost always has charge of the poultry flock.
Many farm women help to cultivate the smaller truck
gardens and also to sell the products. In numerous
cases the woman is an independent producer, raising
flowers, fruits, and vegetables for sale or marketing
honey, eggs, cheese, or butter to add to the family income. Various home industries have also proved
profitable to farm women, such as baking cakes or
bread for sale, canning, making hooked rugs, baskets,
and many other articles for which wild-growing
materials are to be had for the taking.

Many of these home industries are being fostered by
the coöperative extension organization which I represent. To those unfamiliar with this branch of the work
of the United States Department of Agriculture, I
should explain that in connection with the agricultural
or "land-grant" college in each State, there is a teaching group known as the "extension division" which is
charged with carrying directly to the farmer the most
desirable methods for the conduct of the farm business,
and to the farm women whatever information the
science of home economics has found to be useful and
helpful in the home. The boys and girls on the farm
are encouraged by special agents, also part of the extension force, to joint what are called the 4-H clubs.
In these they learn good methods of farming and farm
homemaking to apply to both their present and future
ways of doing things. These three types of extension
workers,—"county agents," who deal with agricultural
problems; "home demonstration agents," who work
with women and girls, and "club agents" who organize

and teach the boys and girls,—are jointly paid by the agricultural college and the United States Department of Agriculture. Their progress and appropriations are all scrutinized in Washington as well as in the State in which they work.

The presence of an extension agent in a rural community is a call to action. Farmers and farm women are brought together in committees and groups. They think through their individual farm, home, and community problems; they undertake things coöperatively. They organize associations, conduct meetings, make reports, put on demonstrations, write news items, make speeches, analyze local conditions, make surveys. They get together in large undertakings.

### The Farm Woman Goes into Business

It has been the observation of the extension workers in most parts of rural United States that the dearth of conveniences and labor-saving devices with which many farm women contend is due to lack of sufficient cash income for buying them. While an astonishing amount of ingenuity and invention is displayed in overcoming the lack of the facilities that every city woman enjoys, it has been clear that the farm woman would not be released from much needless drudgery until she had enough money to provide herself with such household helps as running water, electricity, good tools and efficient equipment. Consequently much encouragement has been given to fostering any industries that promise an increase in cash income. Extension workers have also helped with the marketing problems of these women, introducing curb and club markets, demonstrating how wayside stands can be made effective and how to market by parcel post. One woman writes: "The money I get from the market is buying things for the comfort of my family; it has installed water in the kitchen, it has bought a Chevrolet car, purebred poultry, two cows, furniture, rugs and clothing for myself and other members of my family. My plans for next year are to get a new dining-room suite, furnish a bed room for my son and finish some work on the house."

And another says: "The money I made on the market was for the comfort of my home. I have sold produce to the amount of $644.42."

The story of what the farm woman is accomplishing beggars the telling because the profits which are coming into her treasury are doing so much to revitalize lives, to make over homes, to give incentive where once was drudgery and discouragement. And the story is only half told with the achievements of the farm woman, for it begins with the girls in their clubs who are also capitalizing their smaller talents.

Another woman in checking up her accounts at the end of the summer marketing season declared a profit of $278 on products from her own garden, pantry and poultry yard which she admits would have gone to waste because, as she says, "I didn't realize I had the things."

It is from the standpoint of human economics that the farm woman's new achievements stand the test better than from any other. While she is expanding her daily round of interests and improving the standards of production and marketing she is at the same time injecting the magic of a cash return into what has been considered, if not valueless, at least non-negotiable. And along with increased income and higher standards of living and work, comes the very vital by-product of greater contentment.

In a good many cases the success which crowns the experimental efforts of this new comer in the business field is a dividend on disaster, a cashing in on the silver lining to what looked like a cloud over the sky of the family homestead. One woman, for instance, started out on her career of salesmanship when her husband was ill and unable to do his full-time share in supporting the family. Taking the products of their garden and poultry yard she and her children went to the curb market recently established in a near-by town. The first year, in spite of being kept from market many days by illness, they sold $453.90 worth of products, enough to enable the children to remain in school through the winter. That was the beginning of a successful market venture, which is steadily expanding.

The farm woman as a producer has the great advantage of being at the very hub of production in the primary necessities of life, and the disadvantage of being a long way off of Main Street and Market Street, the highways of consumption. She is beginning to cash in on her advantage and to overcome her disadvantage through establishing markets which tap the stream of consumption at some point—along the side of the road, in the curb of the nearest town, through an exchange, or through the rural mail box. A great purpose has been served in opening the markets, as well as in giving the farm wife confidence to offer her products.

The gradual breaking down of the isolation of the farm through the universal adoption of the automobile and the improvement of roads has, of course, been a tremendous factor in offering the farm woman a way out for her wares. Given an appetite whetted by a forty-mile drive, a basket of home-made doughnuts and a jug of fresh cider beneath the bough of a spreading elm tree, and the story becomes a simple one of supply and demand, with profit to the maker of the doughnuts and advantage to the tourist. Many farm women are beginning to see this and go no further than the juncture of the hedge and the highway for their market.

### The Farm Woman Is Learning

American farm women are doing a great deal of thinking. This is an era full of opportunity for the American farm woman when she may undertake and achieve things undreamed of by the farmer's wife and daughter of former years. For the farm woman this awakening to the broader possibilities of life has meant that she has much to learn from the outside world. She knows in a vague way that she would like to have the culture and enjoyment of her city sister, and she turns to the extension worker and other agencies to learn how to get more comfort and leisure for her family.

Obviously, there are two kinds of education. One should teach us how to make a living, and the other how to live. Surely these should never be confused in the mind of any man who has the slightest inkling of what culture is. The word "culture" has innumerable definitions, but we may quote one of Matthew Arnold's as being suggestive. He speaks of culture as "a harmonious expansion of all the powers which make the beauty and worth of human nature." The farm woman is gradually getting education in both of these aspects.

She has stepped out of her home to attend the home demonstration club meeting, the short course at the State University; even the recreation camps for farm women are teaching her how to play. She is discovering her own powers of leadership. Modest, quiet women who feared to second a motion in a meeting a few years ago, have now discovered their power and are speaking, presiding and leading in a splendid way. It would seem that every rural community possesses women who can help in the solution of all its problems.

## The Drift from Country to City is Normal

Economists tell us that the constant movement of a certain number of people, especially young people, from rural to urban communities is entirely normal. Provided, of course, that a sufficient proportion of the members of strong families remain at home to renew the stock. In this connection I would like to call to your attention a study made several years ago by the United States Department of Agriculture and described in what is known as Department Bulletin 984. It is entitled "The National Influence of a Single Farm Community." Maps are given to show where various people of this community migrated to, what sort of men and women they became and what they and their children did to enrich the nation. This community had a local academy supported and attended for many years by its farm people so that they had at their very door the means of culture and "the good life" which is so eagerly sought. The author of the study believes that in this bringing of the satisfying things directly into the rural community lies one solution of the problem of keeping the farmer on the farm.

The superior type of farm home which I have been discussing performs indirectly another interesting function in our national life. There is a very marked movement from the city outward—not necessarily to the open country but to the surrounding suburban districts. People who have always lived in rented apartments are finding that it is better to possess a small house not too close to its neighbors, a plot of ground, and some growing and living things—vegetables, flowers, and perhaps some chickens. They bring with them certain city ways, but unconsciously they look to the best type of country home for an example of how to live in their new surroundings. The farm family has an opportunity here to place the emphasis on real values. Simplicity in the home, beauty of surroundings, and trained skill in homemaking are some of the points the new suburban dweller learns to value.

## THE FUTURE CONTRIBUTION OF THE FARM FAMILY

The future contribution of the farm family depends to some extent on how important we consider the kind of contribution it has already made and what agencies take part in fostering the attainment of its desires.

It is to be expected that there will be a steady shift of the marginal and unsuccessful farm population to other occupations where managerial qualities are not required, or that they will be hired and directed by the more intelligent modern agriculturists. Standards of living comparable with those in the city are already established in a great many farm communities and these standards are becoming more and more general as time goes on. Farm homes are being made more convenient to live and work in, more books and music are available through libraries, radios and victrolas. Even in the matter of clothes, the country bred man or woman is enabled through easier transportation to see and select practically the same styles as the city stores show. Increased income and a desirable standard of living go hand in hand. It is a nice question whether or not a better income leads to a better standard or results from striving for a better standard. In other words, it may merely be a condition which makes possible the attainment of recognized desires. These desires no doubt stimulate the effort to increase the income.

The attainment of this desirable mode of life by the farm family is being helped by many public agencies. To mention but a few: The Federal Farm Board, the Federal Board of Vocational Education, the Bureau of Education, the Public Health Service, the Red Cross, Better Homes in America, and the United States Department of Agriculture. Of course, I am most familiar with the last. You may be interested in a brief outline of what we are doing that is of benefit to the farm home.

Indirectly, a number of the bureaus and services of the department assist the homemaker with her problems, but the two branches which are directly helpful are the Bureau of Home Economics and the extension work for farm women and girls.

The Bureau of Home Economics is organized for scientific research in the problems of the home. It does not have field workers. At present it has on its scientific staff about 30 specialists, in foods, nutrition, clothing, textiles, budgets, and other economic problems of the home. They are working on such practical problems as home canning, what to feed the family to insure the best possible nutrition, home baking, vitamins in foods, how to judge the wearing quality of textiles, home laundry methods, stain removal from fabrics, household budgets, and time schedules for the homemaker.

Home demonstration for women and girls is one of the phases of agricultural extension work. Its scope is educational, and its workers are trained home economics teachers. They endeavor to stimulate interest in improved home practices, organize community groups of farm women, and assist in developing programs for these groups that shall contribute toward a more efficient, comfortable, healthful, and satisfying farm life.

Whatever is taught in extension work in home economics is part of a carefully worked out plan based on the known wishes of the farm women themselves, and related to the general agricultural and home study program of the county. A farm woman can find an opportunity to learn something about almost any subject that interests her from hens to hats, and when she takes part in a definite program offering logical steps from one feature to another, she is likely to get the most benefit and develop into an unusually capable community leader.

Many popular bulletins on household subjects are issued by the department. These are usually prepared by members of the staff of the Bureau of Home Economics, and are the result of research or compilation of the best available data on any given subject. Some of the most recent are: "Selection of Cotton Fabrics," "Home Baking," "Canning Fruits and Vegetables at Home," "Stain Removal from Fabrics," "Methods and Equipment for Home Laundering," "Convenient Kitchens," "Planning Your Family Expenditures," and various leaflets on cooking beef, lamb, pork and eggs, as well as those on clothing children and training them in good food habits. The Bureau of Home Economics also handles a large correspondence with individuals seeking home economics information. A great many short newspaper articles are issued on household subjects, and the new radio service includes a section called "Housekeepers Chat," which provides radio stations all over the country with material of interest to homemakers.

It would be difficult to enumerate without omission all of the activities of other bureaus of the department that affect home interests. To mention but a few of them: The Bureau of Public Roads is concerned with home sanitation, sewage disposal, heating plants, plumbing, and farm architecture; the Bureau of Chemistry has various laboratories working on commercial food practices, one on leather and paint, and, up to the present, has administered the Food and Drugs Act; the Bureau of Animal Industry, similarly, has been in charge of the federal meat inspection, and the development of all farm practices affecting livestock, including poultry, hence meat and poultry products as food; the Bureau of Dairying is interested in the increased use of milk and milk products; the province of the Bureau of Plant Industry is the growing, storing, and preservation of food plants, and also the beautification of the farmstead through flowers and landscaping; the Bureau of Entomology helps the homemaker deal with insect pests of the household; the Biological Survey not only shows her how to get rid of rats and mice, but also how to raise rabbits or buy a fur coat; the Bureau of Agricultural Economics is working on improved practices in the standardization and distribution of food products, studying standards of living on farms, and is interested in all community activities; through motion pictures, lantern slides, exhibits, and many photographs, home economics information is also carried visually to the people who need it.

## CONCLUSION

The number of farm homes in the future may be smaller than in the past, but agricultural production will be about the same because of the greater intelligence of the families engaged in it. After all, the great contribution of the farm family is the *quality* of its human products—their resourcefulness, creative ability, physical vigor and potential leadership. As Dr. C. B. Smith has said: "The future rural home and the future rural life should be the most attractive home and the most attractive life of all the ages, a home the child leaves with regret and returns to with outstretched arms, a home of plenty—fields, flocks, orchards, gardens—of beauty and grace, where intelligence, hospitality, culture, and happiness abound. The folks who feed and clothe the nation and furnish the revivifying blood of our urban population are entitled to no less. It is on the way. This vision is all a part of the extension program of the agricultural colleges, the United States Department of Agriculture and the farmers coöperating and is being carried out under your own eyes throughout the whole nation this day."

# HOUSING THE FARM FAMILY

## BY JULIA D. CONNOR

The nature of the community depends upon the kind of families that comprise it, and the nature of the families depends upon the kind of homes in which they live.

There is an old saying, "God made the country and men made the town." Man in his vanity sometimes thinks that his work outshines that of the Creator, but we know that when country folks can attain the most worthwhile of city advantages, there is no comparison between the city and country as a place to live, for rural conditions at their best furnish an opportunity for home life of the highest type. It is much easier to make the house in the open country, however humble it may be, into a real home than it is the tenement, flat, apartment or rented house of the city. Congestion of cities does not make for the highest type of home life, nor can all the advantages of which the city may boast compensate for the wide areas, natural beauty and opportunities for development which are offered by the farm home. President Hoover has said, "The farm is more than a business; it is a state of living." The farm home stands for the business and social life of the family, offering far greater opportunities for association of parents and children than the city home, which has in many cases, become little more than a parking place. But the farm home like the city home is not without its rivals. With good roads and ready means of transportation to the city, it must now compete with the outside attractions life possesses.

In order, therefore, to insure that strong, wholesome family life which is so necessary to the development of the community and the safety of the State and Nation, it is important that we do all in our power to preserve in both city and country the strength of home life. This means that the people who live in farm homes must be happy, healthy, and contented. It means that their homes must be attractive and as stated by Dr. James Ford, who is Director of Better Homes in America and Professor of Social Ethics at Harvard, in a paper before The Academy of Political and Social Sciences, "To return from school or from the day's work to a dwelling of three or four dull, malodorous rooms, and then to find nothing of beauty or charm, no convenient place to read or play or entertain one's friends, is likely to lead either to sullen indolence or to profound discontent." Doctor Ford points out that this gives a thirsting to the individual for the excitements which the night life may offer where he is confronted with the agencies of commercial recreation, drink or vice and says: "Reduced in physical and moral resistance by the condition of the dwelling he calls home and obsessed with a justifiable desire for gayety and adventure and release from the thralldom of intolerable circumstance it is scarcely strange if he succumbs to moral hazards and becomes involved in

9

socially undesirable or anti-social activity."

Someone else has said, "Let us be done with those ugly houses that consciously or unconsciously offend us, fill us with unrest and longings that drive the young people to the city and make farm living drab existence instead of rich life."

Good housing must meet certain standards and should provide for every family, irrespective of occupation or income, a type of home which would be healthful, safe and comfortable. It should provide a workshop for this most important business of homemaking, at least as convenient as the workshop where other industries are carried on. The mother, who must be both homemaker and housekeeper, cannot be expected to give much time or thought to the social and moral life of her family if she is a victim of that needless drudgery which characterizes so many of the homes of the nation.

Not the least important of the attributes of good housing is beauty. The drawing power of artistic beauty should be well known in this country. The saloon men of a few years ago knew it. Only recently I was entertained in a tea room in a New England city which I was informed had been a bar room in pre-Volstead days. The walls of the room were beautifully paneled with Circassian walnut, the ceilings covered with mural paintings, and the room lighted with fixtures by Tiffany. Theatrical and movie men know it. Our merchants and business men know it. When will the homemakers of our country learn that beauty in the home will draw to the home and hold there as effectively as anywhere? Many homes have been wrecked because of untidiness, worn nerves, and the loss of comeliness incident to drudgery of keeping the house without proper facilities. Only a few weeks ago, the chairman of a local Better Homes Committee reported that the house which her committee had used as a reconditioning demonstration had been the neglected home of a father and two sons who had been deserted by the wife and mother, and after reconditioning it proved so attractive that it reunited a family who took it as their home.

Dr. Seaman Knapp, who first furnished the vision and inspiration for home demonstration work wrote, "The greatest schools for the human race are our homes and the common schools—greatest in amount and value of the knowledge acquired. A country home, be it ever so plain, with a father and mother of sense and gentle culture, is nature's university, and is more richly endowed for the training of youth than Yale or Harvard." At another time he said, "The world's most important school is the home and the small farm."

Dr. Ray Lyman Wilbur, Secretary of the Interior, and President of Better Homes in America, in a recent address before the Convention of the National Congress of Parents and Teachers, said, "We can only hold our democracy together if we have a contributing, responsible, educated, obedient, loyal and interested citizenship where each thinks for himself but merges his independent efforts with those of his neighbors. Here in America we have a considerable percentage of such citizenship in all of our communities. Where that percentage is high, we have good public order, economical management of public affairs, free from abuse, and conditions generally favorable for the comfort and happiness of human beings. The home as we know it in America is basic to such citizenship. Such citizenship is basic to permanence in our Government. The mother is basic in such a home. In other words, in this great republic we must depend upon the American mother and the home which she maintains for her children if we are to have permanence and security.

"It is then not only important but vital to our future to assist our women in the maintenance of homes of such a character that in them the boys and girls will go through those experiences which lead to their development as contributing citizens."

If the farm home is to fulfill its purpose and serve as the training center for the farm family, the mother who is at the same time housekeeper and homemaker, must be provided with time enough and strength enough for the job. She is entitled to that freedom, now accessible to her, which comes through the use of modern equipment. Now the conveniences of home are not restricted to city dwellers as in the past when water systems, electric lights and attractive surroundings were accessible only to the city. Such conveniences are accessible also to the farm home and every year sees more modern homes built in the country. The farm homemaker, like her city sister, has learned the many things that can be done with electricity and gas. The adaptation to farm uses of labor-saving equipment, such as electric light and power plants, gas-light plants, water systems, heating plants, sewage disposal systems, has served to create a desire for more home comforts and has brought about a great change in living conditions on farms. At the present time the farm home can be fully as modern as the best city home.

It was to bring to the homemakers of the nation, both of the city and country, a knowledge of high standards of home life and to give direct to them the training which will help to attain those standards that Better Homes in America was organized to promote.

Better Homes in America is an educational institution, which was founded in 1923, with Herbert Hoover, then Secretary of Commerce, as its President. From that time to this, the President has not relaxed his keen interest in the plan and progress of the work and continues to serve as Honorary President of the organization. Dr. Ray Lyman Wilbur, Secretary of the Interior, has been appointed President, to succeed Mr. Hoover, while the work of the organization is carried on under the active direction of Dr. James Ford. Begun as a private enterprise, the movement became a force of such importance in helping the American people to higher standards of housing and home life that at the close of 1923 it was reorganized on a permanent basis, and arrangements were made to have the work financed from public gifts. It was incorporated for the purpose of education and public service, and the headquarters of the movement were set up in Washington, D. C.

The purposes of the Better Homes movement are:

1. To make accessible to all citizens knowledge of high standards in house building, home furnishing, and home life.

2. To encourage the building of sound, beautiful, single-family houses; and to encourage the reconditioning and remodeling of old houses.

Although peculiar conditions in certain places, and the circumstances of certain families make it necessary that there shall be apartments and tenements, it is strongly felt that the happiest and most wholesome home life is possible for a family with growing children only in a detached, single-family house. Such a house, then, should be the American ideal, and should be made accessible to all American families.

3. To encourage general study of the housing problem and of problems of family life, and to help each community to benefit from its study.

4. To encourage thrift for home ownership, and to spread knowledge of methods of financing the purchase or building of a home.

5. To encourage the furnishing of homes economically and in good taste.

6. To supply knowledge of the means of eliminating drudgery and waste of effort in housekeeping, and to spread information about public agencies which will assist housekeepers in their problems.

7. To encourage the establishment of courses of instruction in home economics in the public schools, and particularly the construction of home-economics cottages and home-management houses where girls in our

public schools and colleges may, by actual practice, learn the best methods of conducting household operations and of homemaking.

8. To encourage the building of small houses by boys of vocational schools or vocational classes of public schools, and instruction in house upkeep and repair; so that the boys of the community may acquire an intelligent interest in the problems of householding and home ownership.

9. To promote the improvement of house lots, yards, and neighborhoods, and to encourage the making of home gardens and home playgrounds.

10. To extend knowledge of the ways of making home life happier, through the development of home music, home play, home arts and crafts, and the home library.

11. To encourage special study and discussion of the problem of character building in the home.

These purposes are accomplished through the efforts of local Better Homes committees, with the advice and assistance of the Washington office. That office serves also as a clearing house of sources of information on home problems; conducts research on the subject of home improvement; and seeks to coördinate the activities of national, state, and local organizations which deal with any aspect of home life.

# V

## THE COUNTRY SCHOOL WITH
## A SOCIAL VISION

# FUNDAMENTAL NEEDS OF THE
# COUNTRY SCHOOL

## BY EDGAR WALLACE KNIGHT

Even a glance at public education in the United States reveals many glaring inequalities set heavily against the rural areas. These inequalities appear in the provisions for school support, in the length of school terms, in buildings, grounds, and equipment, in teachers, in materials and methods of instruction, and in supervision and direction. In these and other features of public educational work appears the lack of the uniform and general school system which every state constitution in its provisions for education presumably seeks to establish and maintain for all the children. But this mandate of the fundamental laws of the American States has not been obeyed. Thousands of the rural children are grossly discriminated against and denied the educational opportunity to which they are entitled. Public educational practices in the rural sections exhibit not regularity, consistency, and equality, but irregularities, inconsistencies, and inequalities.

Many of the rural schools are attempting the impossible task of providing seven or eight grades of instruction generally under the direction of poorly trained teachers. Most of the children in these schools are in the lower grades. The average size of classes in the upper grades of some of the schools is one to three pupils. There is much retardation, there is much non-attendance, and there is considerable evidence that elimination begins quite early and progresses very rapidly. The older children often quit these poorly equipped schools in which the poorest teachers often seek shelter. Inadequate school buildings and difficult school conditions and poorly trained and ineffective teachers are educational affinities.

Probably few if any features of public education furnish a source of more depressing and humiliating reflection than the physical conditions of many of the schools in the rural sections. Many of them are still marked by nakedness and deformity. Numerous are the comfortless, old-fashioned, box-like buildings, many of them old and in bad repair. Many of the schoolhouses are unhygienic and dangerous and should be condemned as unfit for use. The tiny yards are often unclean, sometimes littered by paper and scraps of lunches, and the facilities for modesty and decency and the protection of health and morals are inadequate or lacking altogether. Sanitary toilets are not often found. The toilets that are provided are not often properly located and almost invariably they are neglected and in poor repair, without screens against flies, almost always filthy, and often they bear inside and out vulgar and obscene markings. There is little instruction in such subjects as physiology, health, hygiene, and sanitation that has passed beyond the academic or mere book stage. Multitudes of the rural schools of the United States are public immoralities, crimes against children.

It is becoming more and more evident to those who study the problems of rural life that agencies concerned with the prevention of disease and the protection and promotion of health among the people of rural areas can perform most effectively and economically by working through the larger and better organized rural schools. Only in the well organized schools with properly trained teachers can adequate instruction be given in such subjects as sanitation and hygiene, personal and public health, the prevention of disease, and the like. The United States Public Health Service insists that the proper foundation for rural health service is through the county health department under the direction of a well qualified whole time county health officer. Approximately seventeen per cent of the total rural population of the United States is supplied with local public health service. But the best conditions are generally found in those states that have placed emphasis on the necessity of professionally trained county superintendents of schools. Enlightened public health service is usually encouraged in counties which are fortunate in their educational leadership. This important field of rural welfare can best be developed through the properly organized and professionally directed rural consolidated school, through which public health departments can most effectively operate and in which adequate health instruction can be given.

There are approximately 160,000 one-teacher schools in the United States at this time and the teachers in them are deficient in training and in educational outlook. Of the 230,000 rural and small town school teachers, approximately 23 per cent, or about 53,000, have had less than two years of study beyond the elementary school. More than one-third of them are not high school graduates. Fully 15,000 have gone no farther than the eighth grade, and at least 5,000, according to recent reports, have completed only the sixth grade or less. More than 4,000,000 of the rural children in the United States are in old fashioned and primitive one-teacher schools.

Schools of this kind do not have and cannot have a social vision. The teachers are not centers of light and leading. Spiritless, uninspired, and uninspiring they grope their way clumsily and aimlessly through the routine and monotony of giving and hearing lessons, which number in some cases thirty-five to forty a day in the one-teacher schools. Many of the teachers are doubtless doing the best they can, as well as their little light will allow. But most of them are without adequate preparation and training and a great many of them are in charge of schools for the first time. They go on from day to day, week to week, and from month to month without any professional help or supervisory guidance whatever from those who know. Chained in their own helplessness they are allowed to warp the plastic minds of little children, many of whom seek and find escape from the dreary surroundings as soon as they are able, probably to become, as they grow older, stubborn opponents to any proposal for schools better than they themselves have known. Most of the teaching in the rural schools is, for these reasons, below acceptable standards and a great deal of it is far below such standards. Superior teaching is not often seen; it is generally lifeless and marked by a lack of acquaintance with modern materials and methods of instruction. The poor preparation of the teachers, the short terms of the schools, the lack of supervision, poor equipment and unwholesome surroundings, and the irregularity of attendance, make many of the rural schools mere makeshifts of educational agencies. Much of the instruction in many of the small rural schools is probably no better today than that found in such schools twenty-five or thirty years ago.

The rural schools suffer seriously from a lack of proper supervision, a defect that reflects itself in the absence among the teachers of a professional attitude, the absence of any observable unity of purpose, and in the absence of any general understanding of educational ideals, objectives, and policies. It reflects itself also in the absence of wholesome community spirit. School societies, parents and teachers' organizations, debating, athletic, library, musical, civic and other clubs are not numerous in the rural areas. The possibilities of making the school the community center have not been realized generally. Few of the agencies now so widely used in progressive urban school systems to unify the educational work of the community and to encourage collective action are being utilized in rural areas. The lack of adequate rural school supervision results, therefore, in much social waste, prevents the public from becoming acquainted with the needs and vitally interested in the problems of the schools, and prevents the school from becoming acquainted with the needs and problems of the community. The value of competent rural school supervision is now recognized in all progressive school systems. Besides greatly improving instruction, supervision increases the children's interest in and appreciation of their school work. It also encourages them to look beyond the conventional subjects taught in the school, enables them to discover interests in new subjects, leads them to wider reading and establishes in them reading habits. It also leads them and their parents to feel the need for improving their school.

Intelligent and effective supervision justifies itself as an agency for unifying the educational work of the county. It enables the county school authorities to gain an intelligent view of the teachers as individuals, it encourages a community to desire and to make effort to get good teachers, and it also encourages and assists the weaker teachers to become stronger. Supervision helps to remove isolation, one of the greatest obstacles to effective educational work in many of the rural schools. Isolation is the mother of many evils, among them retardation and backwardness for pupil, teacher, and community. Sympathetic supervision helps to break down barriers, to foster understanding, and to organize all the forces of the community. Supervision works against provincialism and narrowness and makes for a wider educational and social outlook.

Supervision, probably more than any other single agency, enables the school to become a social center through a fuller use of the school plant, which should and can be made to yield a larger service to the community. In addition to being made an effective teaching center, the properly organized and conducted rural school can become also a recreational, civic, and health center. It can be used for organized play, evening recreational classes, clubs, holiday celebrations, for meetings of Boy Scouts, Campfire Girls, debating activities, mothers' clubs, parent-teachers' associations, for the open forum, for the use of traveling libraries, for purposes of medical inspection and supervision, and for many other activities which the properly organized rural community is now increasingly developing.

In the chaos of county government and the evils of localism are the roots of many of the afflictions which fall so heavily upon rural schools. Considerable educational authority is still vested in local communities and neighborhoods. This practice, maintained by law and strengthened by long tradition, has been sanctioned by the advocates of local self-government since the days of Thomas Jefferson and, because of the deep democratic color which it is believed to wear, still commends itself to wide popular approval.

The theory of local self-government in education served well an earlier period of primitive demands. The district school arose as a small local neighborhood undertaking, to meet local neighborhood needs. It was simple and it was democratic and through its management and control the people could directly express their wishes on education. But the district school arose out of pioneer conditions when the demand for education was simple and easily met and when, in fact, it was no reproach to be illiterate. The conditions out of which this simple system of school administration arose in most American communities have now changed, but in many places the old district still persists, its essential features having undergone but little change since its early days.

Education can never flourish under the small, narrow and artificial district, whose boundary is measured by the length of a child's legs. The district system acts as the deadly upas and withers everything that comes under its shadow. It is largely responsible for the glaring inequalities in education, and these must remain conspicuous so long as the district system remains so strongly protected by law and so comforted and encouraged by misplaced confidence in or devotion to the alleged virtues of local self-government in education. The small school district has not made for real freedom. It has made and even now makes for slavery. The rural children often live under the tyranny of a theory which blocks their path to educational opportunity. It strangles suggestions for new ways of providing better schools. The district system is democracy gone to seed; it is an evil inheritance from the past.

Other evils which have their roots in localism appear in conditions of the physical equipment of the schools. The design and construction of schoolhouses call for a professional direction which is essential to an intelligent educational program but which is not acknowledged as essential by communities which have had little opportunity to learn the difference between a good and safe schoolhouse and a poor and unsafe one. When the design and construction of a school building are left to the whims of a locality ignorant of the best principles of schoolhouse planning, the children are likely to be deprived of advantages to which they are by right entitled and the tax-payers are likely to be defrauded of honest measure.

These evils cannot be removed until closer professional and supervisory direction and oversight are exercised than can be possible under the loose-jointed practices that now prevail. And such direction and oversight by the state are presumably impossible until that unit of administration acknowledges its obligation to provide for every child in the state a good school building. Too often has the state denied this responsibility and left to the counties the burden of building schoolhouses, and this task these units of government have pressed upon the districts, many of which are too feeble to meet them.

These evils can be removed and justice can be more nearly done the children of rural areas only through the use of the real county unit of school support and control. The obstacles which inhere in and grow out of the district system can be broken down most readily by the county unit, which may be properly compared with the modern methods of management found increasingly today in all large business enterprises. The district system, on the other hand, is a relic of pioneer days.

The county unit is now accepted as fundamental to
the permanent growth and improvement of rural educational affairs.

The proper consolidation of all the schools under
the county as the unit means that all property is equally
taxed for school purposes, all schools are operated for
the same length of term, the salaries of the teachers
are established on the same schedule, district lines and
community jealousies disappear, and the financial support and the supervision of instruction of all the
schools, no matter where they may be located, are more
certain and effective than under the district system.
Under the county unit plan men and women of ability
and educational interests are more likely to have membership on the board of education. The position of
county board member then commands larger respect
than under the district plan and affords opportunity
for a more valuable educational service to a larger
number of people. Under the county unit plan all
schools have a higher type of administrative management than is possible under the district system.

The county unit plan brings to the rural schools also
a professional service which the district system can
never afford. Under it a program for supervision of the
highest quality of effectiveness is organized and
executed. Effective classroom instruction, now one of
the largest needs of the rural schools, is increased.
Central control, improved organization, and a high
type of educational leadership, which are found in the
county unit system, create public sentiment in behalf
of the development of standard secondary schools,

which are now lacking in many rural sections, in part because the district system has too long been depended upon to provide them. Under the district system educational affairs are handled slowly, uncertainly, and generally very ineffectively.

Under the properly organized and supported county unit system, the teachers occupy positions of larger public esteem in the community and enjoy a respect which is more nearly comparable to that enjoyed by workers in other professions. The teacher is no longer the hired hand of the neighborhood but the educational representative of a well-ordered school system. The teacher works under professional instructions from the county superintendent and not according to the whims of Trustee Jones or Trustee Smith. There is an increased professional respect, employment is more nearly permanent, salaries are larger, living conditions for the teachers are superior, and improved teaching service results, and the social-mindedness of the community increases.

It appears that the minimum standards by which the rural school can gain and keep a broad social perspective are:

1. A larger unit of support and direction than that which now exists in such wide practice under what is in reality the old district system. It even seems desirable that the smallest legally allowable unit for taxation for schools should be the county. Local taxation in arbitrarily formed districts, which are often weak and small, should be discouraged if not prohibited by law. Localism cannot promote public educational

progress or wholesome educational sentiment, nor can it longer be justified even as a temporary expedient. It encourages selfishness and provincialism.

2. The general administration, direction and supervision of the public schools and other educational interests of the county such as libraries should be vested in a stronger and more effective county board of educational control.

3. A better type of county superintendent is needed. It cannot be emphasized too often or too strongly that the county superintendent of schools is strategically the most important of all the county officers. Potentially he is the most influential. He should bear to the county a relationship similar to that which the state superintendent should hold to the state. He is the central figure of all public educational agencies of the county and his functions are to initiate, establish, and maintain proper relationships among such agencies. He should, therefore, be an able and well trained educational leader and executive and chosen for administrative and professional fitness, rather than for political purposes. Interest should center not so much in the officer as in the office, not in the superintendent but in the superintendency. In most American states the office of county superintendent of public schools needs to be given a new meaning and a new life. Under the present arrangement he will continue to be the clerk and the political appendage which tradition and an archaic system have made him, and as such he must continue to stand stubbornly in the way of educational progress.

4. Closer and more effective supervision is needed. One large secret of better educational work in urban communities is found in better supervision of the urban schools. The compactness of organization aids coördination and directness and promotes coöperation of teachers, school officials, and the public generally. The rural teacher suffers from lack of frequent personal contact with other teachers and is deprived of the stimulation and enthusiasm that come from professional guidance. Provision should be made for supervisory assistance for the superintendent whose professional work is now necessarily incidental, accidental, or haphazard inspection. Adequate provision for such assistance should be made in every county and every county board should be required to provide a special supervisor for the assistance and direction of the teachers and the schools.

5. More nearly rational plans of school consolidation and transportation are needed. Most of the inequalities that now exist in public education can be removed by the consolidation of the small, weak, poorly graded and poorly taught schools into large, strong, well graded schools, properly located, adequately equipped, effectively taught by competent, well-trained teachers. The purpose of the consolidated school is to give larger and better educational service to the community. Intelligent consolidation means a larger taxable area, better buildings and equipment, better teachers, enriched courses of study, better grading and classification of pupils, closer and more intelligent super-

vision, more wholesome and attractive community spirit. The minimum standard for rural school consolidation and transportation requires the school authori-, ties to consider the needs of the county at large rather than the desires of special localities.

These standards must be met before the typical country school can gain a social vision.

# SOCIAL VISION AND RURAL EDUCATION

## BY FANNIE WYCHE DUNN

The rural school, like any other school, is a social institution, set up and maintained by the coöperative endeavor of a society, a group of individuals working together in pursuit of a common interest which is more or less recognized by all members of that society. The initiation or establishment of a school is always a definitely conscious act on the part of a community. After its establishment it is likely, in time, to become a habitual and unconsidered routine, even to the community which first set it up. Meantime, with a widening of communities of interest, its welfare may have become a matter of significance to more remote social groups, who, however, remain unaware of its relation to their own progress. Both the narrower and the wider community may handicap the school by the neglect which results from accustomedness or by actual misunderstanding or misapprehension of the stage of development at which it has arrived or should have arrived. This is, indeed, just what is happening today. The rural school, as a social institution, is in a state of retarded development, either because it occupies the blind spot in the social eye, or because the vision of society is myopic, or both.

There may have been a time when the rural school was of important concern only to the immediate neighborhood which it served, though one doubts this after reading Dr. Galpin's study of the part played by the graduates of one rural school in the life, not only of

the whole of its own state, but of the whole nation as
well. Whatever may have been true in the past, when
the neighborhood was to a large extent a self sufficient
community, it is certain that today, when we have almost annihilated the barriers of space and time which
once separated contemporary social groups, the rural
school functions significantly, not merely for its immediate clientele, the rural population, but for every
other social group which forms, with the rural population, a larger community.

If I may be permitted to do so, I should like for the
purposes of this paper, to limit the term rural, as I
shall use it, to include only the population living on
farms. In my judgment, one handicap to constructive
thinking about the rural school is too broad an in-
clusion of the term. On the whole, I am not at all sure
that there is any more in common in the educational
problems of the village, or small town, and the rural
school than there is in those of the village and the
urban school. Just what degree of sparsity of population is required to bring with it the serious handicaps
to education which must be surmounted by the farm
child's school, I am not able to say, but my guess is
that the dividing line is much nearer the village of
1,000 than the 2,500 conventionally accepted. The outstanding problem of rural education is the problem of
educating the farmers' children.

For the states of the South, particularly, the quality
of the farm child's school is outstandingly important,
because the South has the largest proportion of farm
population in the whole nation. Only three states out-

side the South, North and South Dakota and Idaho, have as large a percentage of population on farms as are to be found in the southeastern group of states, including Oklahoma, Kentucky and Virginia on the north, but excluding Florida. Very few, of even informed persons, realize the excessive proportion of farm children in the population of the South. To illustrate, Iowa has 95,000 more people (total population) than Virginia, but Virginia has 97,000 more farm children than Iowa. Minnesota has 440,000 greater population than Alabama, but Alabama has 312,000 more farm children than Minnesota. Wisconsin has 73,000 greater population than North Carolina, but North Carolina has 405,000 more farm children than Wisconsin. Indiana has 35,000 greater population than Georgia, but Georgia has 565,000 more farm children than Indiana. Pennsylvania has 4,000,000 greater population than Texas, but Texas has 800,000 more farm children than Pennsylvania. Eleven southern states have one-fourth of the population of the United States, and one-half of all the farm children.

Education is generally recognized today as one of the most potent, if not the most potent, of all factors which affect and determine social progress. What, then, may a state or a section hope for in future prowess if it remains blinded or shortsighted with regard to the education of so large a proportion of its children? The states of the South rank, in educational provision, at the bottom of the national roll. Yet it is very doubtful if the city schools of the South are significantly inferior to city schools the nation over, as it is doubtful if the rural schools of the South are strikingly inferior to rural schools in general. That the average educational level is low is certainly to be explained in large part by the proportion of the disadvantaged type of school situation in its total composition.

This statement is not made with any view of excusing or justifying the South for its low educational rank. Excuse or justification has no value in obviating the inevitable consequences of educational neglect. The South, for all its notable progress in the last quarter century, is dragging in the forward march of events because of educational deficiency. It may salve our self respect to be able to attribute the educational shortages of the present generation to the results of a devastating war. But we must be purblind indeed if we expect mere excuses to put the next generation in step with the rest of the nation. Unless the South is content to remain the tag end of the procession, it must make adequate provision for education of all its children, and this means that it must concern itself with rural education as it never has done in the past. I am not ignorant of the greater vocal attention given to the rural school in recent years, but I seriously question whether it has been more substantial or more productive than the vocal attention extended to agriculture during a political campaign.

If states so largely rural as those of the South are to provide educational facilities adequate to safeguard their future, the city people of the state, and the educational leadership, including all the faculties of its higher institutions and all its state departments of education must see the rural school for what it is and what it might be. I venture the guess that the urban southerner or the southern educational leader who has given any real study to the rural school problem of his section is at least as rare as he who has given any real study to the negro problem.

In truth we need a rural school with a social vision, but I myself would interpret this to mean particularly the need of a social vision back of the school. We have heard a great deal of the need of social vision within the rural school, and this has ordinarily been understood to mean the leadership of a rural teacher who would exert the influence and provide the services which in a larger community would occupy the full time of five or six agencies. Especially has there been expected of this super-teacher a large degree of benefit to the adult community. Various writers have urged upon the rural school—by which is usually understood the rural teacher—the modest tasks of "helping solve the farmers' economic problems," "educating them in modern methods of agriculture and business management," providing "a center of educational and social life not alone for children, but for grownups," "preserving the natural scenery of the community," "conserving motherhood, as well as child life and girlhood," "making all country life more scientific and more contented," and indeed, "building civilization in every part that is not receiving adequate attention from other agencies."

Such statements as these certainly suggest a need of greater social vision with respect to the rural school. They indicate, however, a dawning realization of the futility and barrenness of experience offered by a large per cent of rural schools, and a recognition that a school, if it achieves its social purpose, must be a community builder and a social center. But it is a builder of a citadel of new stones, which are sound, sturdy, wholesome young lives, reared in place of the crumbling rubble of their fathers', and it is a social center in that it draws into itself all the vital activities and achievements of society and uses them as food and exercise for the expanding of its pupils' lives. "The only way to prepare for social life is to engage in social life. . . . Interest in community welfare, an interest that is intellectual and practical, as well as emotional—an interest, that is to say, in perceiving whatever makes for social order and progress, and in carrying these principles into execution—is the moral habit to which all the special school habits must be related if they are to be animated by the breath of life."

The rural school today is in serious need of a vision of its unique service as a social institution. It, and it alone is charged with the task of enabling the farm child to realize his highest potentialities as a member of society. This is its primary function, to which all others are subordinate or incidental. The state, if it is to protect its own future, must bring to the service of this school as expert direction and as generous financial support as is needed to enable it to perform its functions adequately. The present provision is lamentably deficient and it is the state itself which must pay for the results of this deficiency in the future if it does not pay for its removal in the present.

# VI

# COUNTRY COMMUNITY LIFE

# LITTLE COUNTRY TOWNS AND WHAT THEY MAY DO FOR THEIR SURROUNDING TRADE AREAS

## BY NEWELL LeROY SIMS

Little country towns include villages ranging in size from about 250 to 3,000 population. Their trade areas have in them about an equal number of farmers. Villages no longer dominate the surrounding areas with the assurance that once they had. New conditions are altering relations.

It seems as though a crisis is impending in the life of village communities. They have been caught in the midst of conflicting forces, some of which are constructive, while others are destructive in effect. Of the first there are, for instance, such things as the rapid growth of village population in contrast to that of the farms, the focusing of rural activities by the gravitation of crafts and crossroad services to village centers, and some hints that urban industries will tend to decentralize and scatter out into the villages. On the destructive side there is a definite trend of business away from the smaller to the larger towns with the widening of markets. At the same time urban domination is on the increase through chain stores, and commercial organizations that tie local dealers to city practices, while over all is the growing competition of villages with one another as a result of the automobile.

In the midst of these cross currents the little town needs to get its exact bearings both with respect to the city and to the country. Traditionally, it has always looked to the city for guidance, but actually, it is beginning to find that agriculture is its sustenance. With the realization that farming is its basic industry, a new slogan might therefore be, "We encourage our farmers" instead of the old widely blazoned sign-board, "We solicit factories."

A correct orientation of the village will disclose the fact of complete interdependence of itself and its farm area. The latter needs the village very much, but the village needs its farmers a whole lot more. In fact, this dependence upon the farms is much closer than any dependence upon the cities.

Again it will be disclosed that the prevalent relations with the farms are not generally satisfactory. In a few cases there will be cordial coöperation; in more conflict; and in the majority of cases, indifference or neutrality. The latter *laissez faire* state may easily drift into open conflict without much provocation.

It will be further disclosed that the village is engaged in a competition with cities which it is failing to meet to the satisfaction of its farmers.

Finally, it will be seen that farmers are not as firmly attached to one trade center as they used to be when horses and dirt roads prevailed, but that they are now divided in their interests between several small towns and perhaps between small towns as a class and the larger towns and cities.

Squarely facing these circumstances, what program may the little town adopt? Clearly, if mutual good will with its trade area does not already exist, that should first be established. The problem is really not what may the town do for the farmers, but what the town and the farmers together may do as a community. It is futile to talk about benevolent villagism when only mutuality will avail. Unless there is complete confidence and understanding there will be little coöperation and little accomplished. And the evidence seems to indicate a pretty general lack of mutuality. The prevalent relation is one of indifference if not antagonism. The promotion of harmony is therefore the first item on the program.

The village group is rightly thought of as the one to take the initiative in seeking more cordial relations. It is better prepared to do it than the farm group, for the village is compact and can get unified action and organization more effectively. An aggressive attitude on the part of the village, however, often thwarts its purpose. It puts the farmers on guard against the advances. Hence the village can do nothing for or with its farmers, until it has disarmed suspicion. This is not always easy to do. It takes tact and social resourcefulness, qualities for which rural people are none too famous. The end cannot usually be secured by the conventional methods of welcome signs, band concerts, free movies, and prize drawings. Methods less mercenary and more winsome should be employed. These should involve the farmers and villagers in doing something together with their hands and minds. People will hardly remain at logger heads if engaged in mutual activities. Community fairs, picnics, banquets and field days have some merit. Anything indeed that will get farmers and villagers together on a cordial common basis with the commercial motive left out will avail much. I have great faith in the procedure that induces people to talk, eat, and play together, since coöperation in weightier matters is thus often engendered. For those who will pool their activities in small things will learn how to do so for larger stakes in the end.

One canon should always be observed. It is that harmony can hardly be securely established and maintained unless the principle of equality between town and country is respected. The town must not patronize. It cannot dominate. If anything, it should assume that if it would be the greater, it will have to be the lesser in spirit. We are told, for instance, of a Georgia village that came to a full realization that agriculture was its biggest industry and then proceeded to act accordingly by putting the farmers in control of its Board of Trade in the ratio of nine farmers to four villagers. This case illustrates a principle that the village should respect in its general organization scheme if it would succeed in coöperating with its farmers.

The community having secured the desired harmony and degree of coöperation, the next step can be something more tangible. That step may well be an analysis of its agricultural resources. For this project all available expert advice should be mobilized in order to find out what the conditions are and what improvements are possible. A similar analysis of village enterprises will also need to be made to see whether the right kind of service is being rendered and whether it is efficient or not.

By such an analysis every community will discover its limitations as well as its strength, what to avoid and what to pursue. Such knowledge ought to give clear vision and considerable incentive to the realization of improved conditions. It will not, however, remove the many obstacles that hinder social action. But it will at least challenge the community in a wholesome way.

A generous program of this sort before it can have meaning will have to come down to specific projects. These will involve economic, educational, health, recreational and other interests—undertakings that concern every community.

Naturally the foremost interest will be the economic. What may be done about this? The analysis of resources already suggested should reveal possible projects. In many cases, no doubt, the community will discover how to diversify crops advantageously. This will apply especially to one crop regions and notably to Southern communities. From the cotton belt, for example, comes the report of a village that put on a campaign for crop diversification with good results. In place of cotton alone, the farmers were induced to grow tobacco, tomatoes, garden produce, and poultry, both to their own and to the town's profit.

In other sections everything may be gained by encouraging more specialization. Some particular crop may be featured or some special breed of livestock or poultry adopted. There are doubtless neglected opportunities of this sort in almost every locality. Geographic specialization is economically sound and it tends to foster local pride and community solidarity. It is related of a Wyoming stock-raising community that, when it was hard hit by ruinously low prices, it turned to another specialty and raised turkeys. In this new line it excelled and has come to be an important turkey growing center for the Chicago market.

The organization and management of farms is possible of great improvement in virtually every locality. Here is a legitimate field for action as attested by the experience of a group of Illinois farmers. Some two hundred of them in one area joined in a scheme for bettering their enterprises. Experts were employed to study and analyze the operation of each farm unit. The weak and the strong, the winning and the losing methods were thus brought to light, and after three years' effort, the level of efficiency was raised in a gratifying measure. Almost any town-country community could profitably launch some such plan for improving the management of its farms. A bank at Champaign, Illinois, is reported to have under its management thirty-two farms consisting of 7,500 acres of land. Each farm is operated as a unit, but an expert agriculturist is in charge of the management of all. Why could not this idea be carried out at least for demonstration purposes on a coöperative basis by the town-farm community?

On the part of the village the development of manufacturing of farm products is often feasible and desirable. In the case of the cotton-belt town that featured diversification, there was also the promotion of a tomato-packing and storage plant, together with a cannery. Without these the new crops would hardly have been profitable.

Obviously the local processing of farm stuff has decided limitations. In dairy, poultry, and fruit and vegetable growing regions it applies as it does not where the great staples dominate. However, in so far as practical, I believe it to be a sound policy for a community to keep as much of the processing of farm products as near the farms as possible. At least, this is the way the community is likely to profit most.

Another activity the village may foster among its farmers is coöperative buying and selling. Normally this is not done. Village tradesmen array themselves with the cities against coöperation while chain stores, mail-order houses and other city-serving agencies make merry victimizing villagers and farmers alike. One wonders if villagers are not blind as to their manifest destiny. For the trend points to their becoming simply hired clerks in local chain stores and branch offices of urban concerns. Hence in self-preservation the villagers might better join hands with the farmers and become the managers of coöperative enterprises. The future would thus be made more secure for many local dealers. Moreover, economically, farmers' coöperatives ought not to be so disadvantageous to the village as some think. For the latter's function is that of a distributing center and coöperation will not destroy this function. If, however, coöperation gives the farmers more money in the long run, it will mean the importation of more goods to be distributed and hence increase the volume of trade at the center. Thus villagers as well as farmers will stand to gain. From here and there we gather reports of tradesmen who are beginning to see the situation in this light. They are becoming agents for purchasing and distributing farm supplies at the farmers' orders and on a commission basis. If this be not exactly coöperation, it looks strongly in that direction.

The field is broad when coöperative possibilities are considered. The little town may well engage in the promotion of whatever organizations of this sort the region will sustain. It may well be the prime mover in finding out what is needed. Let it direct a survey of its trade zone for information about conditions. Let this survey discover the quantity and quality of the products and the trend of production, together with the methods and marketing problems. Let it find out the failures and shortcomings of marketing and the needs, if any, for an association. Let it arrive at some estimate of what an association can accomplish that will be profitable and beneficial. Let it determine in advance whether the volume of business will justify an organization. At the same time, by such a survey, the farmer's attitude toward coöperation may be disclosed and the problems that must be met if a successful association is to be launched can be brought to light and fully reckoned with. In such a rôle as this the village will identify itself with its farmers to its everlasting glory and gain.

In the matter of credit, the village bank may wisely help the farmers over difficult periods. In some Ohio communities it has become the practice of the banks to pay the farmers' taxes and carry the bill till it is convenient for the farmer to pay. Sometimes months pass before collection, but no charge is made for the service. Credit of that sort the farmer often needs and greatly appreciates.

Unquestionably the little town must face more intelligently the collective problem of what businesses it can sustain. Clearly it cannot provide for every need of the community, for it does not have enough people to afford a paying volume of business in all lines. To recognize this and to discourage enterprises that transgress well defined limits is good policy. Certain studies seem to indicate the limits in a number of fields. Probably, if a village does not have a thousand or more people, it can hardly sustain a furniture store, a dry goods store, a shoe store, a millinery store or a jewelry store. With 500 or even less people, it does seem possible, however, to carry on such things as a hardware and implement business, a drug store, a grocery, and possibly a bank. It is perhaps one of the most important tasks of the little town to eliminate, if possible, needless duplication of its enterprises in the interest of efficiency in community service. I suspect it needs to foster coöperation within its own circle to that end and incidentally to better safeguard its economic future. In other words the socialization of local businesses and organizations is a problem of equal merit with, and greater difficulty than, the socialization of individual farmers and villagers.

Many other types of business service can be developed to meet local conditions. I know, for instance, of a mid-western village that has organized its farmers in a marling association. There are deposits of marl in local lake beds. This is being taken out coöperatively and made available for the soil.

Another development that is spreading rapidly in Michigan is a fire protection scheme. The villagers and farmers together are purchasing fire trucks for their areas. Sometimes the village alone owns the apparatus, but makes its service available to the farmers for an annual fee or membership assessment.

If the little town can carry on harmoniously with its trade zone in business matters, other things of equal importance will be comparatively easy. For town-country difficulties are chiefly economic, not cultural. Perhaps, because of this, cultural projects should come first in any program. Nevertheless, the bread and butter side of life does come first in practice, and, therefore, the order of procedure as I have outlined it. But the other side is no less vital.

Educational problems are obviously significant. What may the village do for its farmers with reference to schools? When consolidation has taken place the village is often the school center. But with incorporated villages such centering is not so common. Villages constitute as a rule independent districts, especially for high school purposes. Discrimination against country children frequently results from this system. The children outside the corporation become tuition pupils in schools over which the farmers have no control. Villages own the schools and sell schooling to the trade zone just as the local merchants sell goods. The schooling may be, but probably is not, exactly what the farm children should have. But they have to take it; for it is all that can be bought locally, and nothing can be done by the farmers to alter it. Such conditions are not altogether just, and the forward looking village will remedy them by extending its high school zone to coincide if possible with its trade area. In some states this is done, but it needs to become a general practice.

However, not every village can maintain a high school. The principle of sufficient volume of business determines what size a community must be for this purpose. At least one hundred pupils and taxable property aggregating from one to two million dollars seem to be necessary for the support of such an institution. A study of this problem in Wisconsin has shown that if all the farm areas tributary to the towns were carved up into efficient high school districts and all the property was taxed for this object, there would be high schools for everybody and the tax rate would be halved or even quartered. Such a scheme ought to appeal both to the villagers who pay high tax rates for schools and to the farmers outside the school districts who pay high tuition rates for the use of the village institution.

Education naturally suggests the library and raises the question of village possibilities in this direction. The American Library Association has estimated that a yearly budget of $4,000 to $5,000 is needed to support any library worthy of the name. On the basis of one dollar per capita this would call for a community of four or five thousand. Obviously the smaller villages cannot afford this institution, if it must be publicly supported. Generally, the county unit seems to be the only practical substitute in such cases. However, in lieu of such provision, it is often possible for villages to organize library services of merit on a very small scale. I know a village that canvassed the entire farm area for dollar memberships, and thus made a beginning of what came to be a well sustained and useful agency for procuring and circulating books and current literature in a community that otherwise would have had nothing of the sort. Unfortunately, our little towns are likely to think of libraries in terms of buildings rather than in terms of books, but books ought logically to be the things first sought.

Health service may be promoted. If the village is large enough, a hospital may be established, but this requires a community of 5,000 to 6,000 people. Even then first class service at a reasonable cost may not be possible. This suggests the advisability of two or more villages coöperating or perhaps enlisting a whole county in the enterprise. Apart from hospitals, every community of a thousand souls should maintain a competent physician who will stress preventive medicine. Country towns are losing their medical men. Only the incompetents, if any, remain. Villages are appealing to the American Medical Association for doctors. Too much competition, overspecialization, starvation, and the lure of a city practice seem to have conspired to entice the doctors away. Local coöperative health associations are being suggested and challenged to save the day. Such organizations may stimulate interest and perhaps put medical service on a new foundation where the local situation demands it. A little Minnesota village of 250 people with about 200 farm families in its area has shown how it can be done in a pinch. They had no doctor. A health association was formed to which each member family paid $24 annual dues in return for all needed service. A physician was procured to come and reside in the village and guaranteed a salary of $3,000. Part of his work consists in educational propaganda for disease prevention.

Rural communities are generally poor in recreational opportunities. The village may cultivate this field also. A ball and picnic ground and a golf course are not beyond reach. And a community house with a good stage is likewise possible where there is vision and leadership. Such facilities will naturally result from a well directed play movement and prove a boon to the community.

Another thing I would include in the village program is the encouragement of art. There is a wide range here, but it will be only the exceptional community that will give art any consideration. The utilities will be so pressing and crowd on to the stage so thick and fast that beauty will have little chance to appear. Nevertheless, there is endless need for the beautification of our villages and countryside. And that town which can effectively stimulate this movement will serve well itself and encourage the larger cause. Efforts in this direction of the little hamlet of Granville, Illinois, are gratifying. Beautification is one item in a larger "Forward movement" program that has received hearty support. Notable things have been achieved in making beautiful its school grounds and interior. It has made art appreciated. Among other things it has established a museum in one room of the high school. Although this may be straying away from the idea of beautification, it suggests to me one thing that our villages in some cases may well do. I saw everywhere in Denmark agricultural museums. Why should not we have them in our villages? Apart from their intrinsic merits, they would serve to foster community pride and tie the village and town together by one more common interest.

The town program as I have conceived it in this discussion ought normally to bring about community-wide organization in the form of a council of institutions and agencies embracing every legitimate interest and activity. By such a pooling of forces a social program can best be planned and realized. The idea is somewhat visionary, I know, for it is easier proposed than realized. But community councils have actually been tried with some success, and who knows to what greater success good leadership may not yet bring them! Idealistically, to strike for a community council first would be the logical thing, but it is rare that society acts logically or even intelligently. Therefore, we have to depend upon the roundabout way, the trial and error method and the emotional appeal, as the surest way to get desirable results. So what ought to come first is usually the last achieved.

# THE OPPORTUNITY OF THE SMALL TOWN: A STUDY OF TOWN AND COUNTRY RELATIONS

## BY JOHN HARRISON KOLB

Every farmer's gate swings open to a road, and good roads lead to towns. Beyond the town lies the city. Therefore, between the country and the city stands the town. It has characteristics of the city and it has characteristics of the country. But it can be said with equal truthfulness that the small town has characteristics and opportunities all its own. Some of these characteristics and opportunities are just being discovered and appreciated by the townspeople themselves and by the students of society.

### How Many Towns Are There?

An interesting preliminary question is, how many towns are there? By special tabulations of the 1920 Census, it was found that there were in the United States about 12,800 incorporated places of between 250 and 2,500 people. But not all villages and towns are incorporated; so all do not appear in the Census reports. By the use of the atlas, 5,500 more places of the same size but unincorporated, were found. Then, including the incorporated places with populations of 2,500 to 5,000, the total comes up to 19,700.

By similar tabulations it was found that nearly seventeen and a half millions live in these towns. This

means that about one out of every six people in the
United States lives in a town. In Wisconsin 24.5 per
cent of the people live in incorporated or unincorporated places of less than 5,000. It means that about
one out of every four people in this state lives in a town.
This would seem to indicate that the town is worthy
of attention.

### What is the Opportunity of the Town?

Briefly put, the opportunities of the town are three.
First, it is a place in which to live. With one out of six
people in the United States and one out of four people
in Wisconsin actually living there, it is evident that
this opportunity is being recognized. Moreover, con-
trary to general belief, their populations are increasing
more rapidly than the nation as a whole.

Second, it is a distribution station for goods and
services. For the Middle West in places of 250 to
2,500, 22 per cent of the men over ten years of age
and gainfully employed are in the trades, and 8½
per cent are in public and professional service. The
clientele for these goods and services is the rural community. Let no one mistake the importance of this opportunity. The farmer and his family are no longer
in the neighborhood stage of economy where they were
dependent upon strictly local agencies. They are in
the midst of a town-country economy. They are dependent upon the goods and services of the town for
the things which go to make up their standards of
living.

Third, it is an assembling station for goods and services. Thirty-four per cent of its men are employed in manufacturing and 12 per cent in transportation. These goods and services are assembled from the producer of original wealth, the farmer. They are assembled and passed on for world consumption. The city is the greatest consumer. Between the country and the city stands the town. This is its real opportunity.

## How the Town Can Realize upon Its Opportunity

The more significant part of this discussion must deal with the question of how the small town can realize upon its opportunities. For this purpose, two propositions are set forth. First, the town may realize upon its opportunities by knowing its constituent service community and secondly, by specializing on reasonable tasks.

## Knowing Its Constituent Community

Surrounding the town is its constituent service community. Its clientele lives out in this community. Its future depends upon its ability to serve well this constituency. But before service can be well rendered, there must be some knowledge of the needs, the characteristics, and the desires of those who live in this tributary territory.

This community area surrounding the town falls naturally into three zones: the first a personal service zone, the second an economic service zone, and the third a specialized service zone. In order to find out just what services are required in each of these zones, 787 farm families in Dane, Walworth, and Waupaca counties were personally visited. Questions were asked regarding "where" and "why" they went for thirteen different kinds of goods and services.

*The Primary or Personal Service Zone.*—In the first zone nearest the town these families reported that they went to the town for the educational service of the elementary or graded school; for the religious service of the church or Bible school; for the sociability service of the club, the lodge, or the social organization; and for the economic service of the general store for groceries, general household and farm supplies and convenience goods. The reasons why they went to this or that particular town center were because they "had friends there," they "knew folks there," "relatives lived there," "it was handy and convenient." One good woman, when urged for her answer regarding the church raised a warning hand and said with bated breath, "why we've always gone there, the old folks are buried there."

Here is a set of town-country relationships which are more or less personal, intimate, or close-by in character. Habit and custom play their parts. The service center is almost taken for granted. The families come into the town without giving it much thought. This situation is particularly true where the towns are quite small, where there is little or no industry, or where there has been no incorporation of the town.

*The Secondary or General Trade Service Zone.*—In the second zone, larger and extending considerably beyond but including the first, is the secondary or general trade zone. In this area the families reported that they frequented the town center for the economic service of the banks, the merchandising establishments, and the marketing agencies; for the educational service of the high school; for the communication service of the telephone, the mail delivery, and the newspaper.

The reasons given for seeking particular towns for these services were "nearest towns," "prices about right," "most convenient place," or "roads are good that way." To be sure these farmers could and frequently did drive through the town in question to other towns. It was not the regular thing, however, so long as "prices, goods, and the service" stayed in line. Then too, they bought from the mail-order houses when the local merchants "didn't treat you right." But it was evident that the relationships of this secondary zone were less personal than the first. They were more economic in character and were more dependent upon the element of accessibility, roads and distances.

*The Third or Specialized Service Zone.*—In the largest zone, called the specialized area, the 787 farm families reported going to the town for the economic service of the larger department store for women's "ready to wear" and for men's good clothes; for the social service of hospital or clinic; for the educational service of a normal or special training school; and for the sociability service of the spectacular motion picture show, musical concert, or theatrical performance.

These families replied that when they went to the town for these services, they went to this or that particular town because there was "a wider variety for selection," because "the service was more expert and professional," and because "the institutions were larger and better." It is evident that here is a set of reasons which are not personal, nor a matter of nearness or convenience, nor yet a question of price or custom. The families were willing to go further, although less frequently, and perhaps to pay more in order to get what they really wanted and could be satisfied with. "You see, I don't get a winter coat every year," one mother said, "so I like to have a variety from which to select." One farmer suggested that he didn't expect to have that sort of an operation again, so he had taken no chances but had gone to the best hospital of which he knew.

But this plan of things for going to one town for certain kinds of services and to other towns for other types of services is not confined to farmers and small towns. Business and professional men and their wives can easily be found in the Madison stores. Madison men and women are seen on trains going to Chicago, even though the Chamber of Commerce may be "putting over" a campaign for "trading in your home town." The old story has truth along with its taunt "the Chicago people go to New York and the New York people go to Paris, while the Paris people go"— well—"write your own ticket."

*One Town in Relation to Other Towns.*—It should now be evident that no one town and its country community can live to itself. Therefore it becomes important not only to know one's own constituent community, but also to know of the relationships to other towns and their communities. A southern Wisconsin farmer, for example, may expect to find a small town of about four or five hundred population within perhaps four or five miles of his home. He may find a center of about a thousand or twelve hundred people about eight or ten miles away, but he will be driving through another smaller place before he gets there. If he wishes to go to a city of five thousand or larger, he may have to drive, on the average, about thirty or thirty-five miles and en route will pass through other smaller centers. These distances, of course, will vary in different sections of the country. In Kansas, it was found that the service centers of about one thousand or twelve hundred population are about fifteen or twenty miles apart. In New York the smaller places are only about five miles distant.

The next question in knowing a community and its service relations to other towns is what happens to the three service zones as the towns become larger or smaller. Suppose one were to start with the town of about a thousand or a little larger. The secondary or general trade zone will be found at its maximum from the standpoint of relative comparisons. For example, it was found in a study of 455 towns, conducted by *Successful Farming*, Des Moines, Iowa, that for those towns of less than 2,000 people, the actual average being 1,033, the percentage of business for all kinds of merchandizing institutions was about 72 per cent from the farm sources. This checks almost exactly with a study of 227 mercantile agencies in similar sized towns in southern Wisconsin. But as the size of town increases or decreases, the proportion of farmer trade to the total business tends to decrease.

As one would expect, the primary or personal service zone is relatively the largest around the smaller centers. It does not differ here very greatly from the secondary area. When it comes to the larger town and especially the city of over five thousand, this primary zone fades out almost completely because the average farmer has few personal contacts through church, club or family tie with the usual city man.

The specialized zone is, of course, largest for the larger towns. For a city center of over 10,000 it may cover a whole county. It will overlap all the zones of smaller towns in such an area. But this specialized area for the smaller town of less than one thousand is not practically important for it does not differ greatly from the general trade or secondary zone.

This whole relationship of town and community with other towns and their communities can be illustrated by the "hill and valley curve." The population of the towns is on the vertical axis, and the distance between the towns is on the horizontal axis. The service zones are indicated by the circles. This relationship can be summarized by the statement that there is a fairly regular relation (the statistician calls it "correlation") between the population of the town center and three other things, namely, the number and kind of service institutions in the town, the distance between this town and other towns, and finally, the size and character of each of its three service zones.

### Specializing on Reasonable Tasks

If the small town would realize upon its opportunity, it must not only begin by knowing its constituent community and its relation to neighboring towns, but it must pass to a second stage, namely, specializing on reasonable tasks. With the picture of the town and its three service zones outlined, it should not be difficult to discover the principle of specialization. In such a scheme of community relations the smaller town cannot reasonably hope for making a success of specializing in dress suits, for example. It can, however, rout the city when it comes to selling overalls. Modern merchandizing needs to take this principle more fully into account. As the changes go on in these community relations and in the means of communication and transportation, changes in service programs will have to be made or certain agencies or even whole towns will find themselves on a sidetrack—out of a job.

The principle of specialization means further, that these tasks adjusted to the needs of constituent communities cannot be worked out selfishly and alone by any one town. If specialization means anything, it means that some of the larger city centers have only recently learned this lesson. Others have long since been operating on this principle. In its direct-mail advertising, one St. Paul concern says, "what you can't buy in your home town, buy at the Golden Rule."

A corollary of the specialization principle is also of importance. One agency or one town center cannot successfully evade responsibility for services which by all reasonable evidence belongs to it. Many local communities have evidently been attempting to do this of late in the matter of organized recreation. The results have not been fortunate, to say the least. They have been turning their young people over to other towns or to private, profit-seeking agencies, where social control was at its minimum instead of adjusting themselves to changed needs and rendering this reasonable service themselves where social control could be at its best.

## SPECIALIZATION PRINCIPLE APPLIED TO THREE INSTITUTIONS

The principle of specializing on reasonable tasks can perhaps be more clearly understood if it can be applied to certain service institutions in which every town and its community are vitally interested. What institutions may a town of a certain size and with certain community relations reasonably expect to make successful? Obviously certain fundamental considerations, such as volume of business, unit costs, overhead, maximum service, will have to be taken into account. Suppose one were to call such other items, *unit requirements*. This idea of unit requirements has long since been recognized in the field of such production institutions as creamery, cheese factory, or gas plant. Is its importance less for social institutions giving community service?

When certain unit requirements can be agreed upon, the next and even the more important question is their translation into community units of people, into service areas, and into social costs. For the sake of illustration, three institutions will be taken. A set of unit requirements for each has been worked out in coöperation with the specialization in each of the fields. The community implications were determined by making a special study of eight Wisconsin counties.

*The High School.*—The service unit for the high school is the pupil. The number cannot fall far below 100 and have a good working unit. To have this many children of high school age, 1,250 people on the average are needed. This number of people, exclusive of places over 3,000 in the eight counties studied, would require an area of about 41 square miles, just a little more than the ordinary township. The total costs per service unit, the pupil, would be $113. Since only 80 per cent of this total was raised from local sources, the costs per capita to the people in the district would be $7.20, and the rate per dollar of the assessed valuation would be 3.7 mills. This is exactly half the rate used by the eight schools. This presupposes that all children of high school age attend school. This opportunity needs to be provided, but with only a 50 per cent attendance, which is about the average, the population and the area of the district would need to be doubled and the rate of taxation could again be cut in half.

*The Library.*—The service unit for the library is the circulating book, and 30,000 is considered the lower limit for good service possibilities. The costs on the basis of this unit would be 13 cents. With a rate of $1.00 per capita, in order to raise a $4,000 budget, an equal number of people would be needed. This many people would require an area of about 133 square miles. If the whole of this budget were to be raised by local taxes, the rate would be only one-half of a mill for the assessed valuation of this area.

*The Hospital.*—The service unit for the hospital is the bed; about 30 beds were considered necessary for one institution. At least $4.00 was to be allowed for the daily per capita cost of the patients. At the rate of five beds per 1,000 people, a population of 6,000 would be needed for the 30-bed hospital. They would distribute themselves over an area of about 200 square miles. The census figures showed about 65 per cent of the hospital costs to be borne by the patients themselves. Therefore, the cost to the community would be $2.10 per capita, or 1.1 mills on the assessed valuation, if this balance were to be raised by local taxation.

The purpose has not been to put emphasis upon these or any other sets of figures but rather upon the necessity of considering unit requirements in any plan of community building—of undertaking and of carrying through reasonable tasks. By all means, farmers and their families want and need their own neighborhood life and organization, but it has become evident by this study of eight counties that they cannot hope to maintain successfully such institutions as high school, library, or hospital, without taking the neighboring towns into their plans. These town centers in Wisconsin appear at too frequent intervals to be left out of the picture when unit requirements are considered. It should further be evident that not every town can reasonably hope to have every sort of an institution needed by its constituency and located within its own corporate limits.

Is it too much to urge, then, that a particular town set itself to doing well the tasks it can reasonably perform and then give at least a measure of coöperation to other neighboring towns or cities for undertaking other tasks which it cannot hope to do successfully?

# VII

## OPEN FORUM ADDRESS

# FARMER-CONTROLLED COMMODITY MARKETING ESSENTIAL TO PROSPEROUS FARMING

## BY BENJAMIN F. YOAKUM

Politics and the farm question have proved bad bed-fellows. Divorce them and wed the two greatest economic forces—Farming and Business. That is what I have urged for twenty years. It is the only way in which farming can ever be placed on a permanently paying basis, and events and public thought are rapidly shaping to that end.

Congress has created a Federal Farm Board with $500,000,000 to retrieve farming from its bankrupt condition and restore it to prosperity. The Board has made a vigorous beginning, is doing the best it can with the imperfect machinery furnished. But the new farm law is inadequate. Stabilization corporations, clearing houses and loans are authorized. But no practical plan is provided by which the vast majority of farmers can organize to control production and marketing under powerful nation-wide marketing organizations distributing and selling their products on the extensive scale which present-day marketing demands. They are represented by "Advisory Commodity Committees," whose compensation is $20 a day when attending meetings. Upon the advice of these powerless and unpaid "Committees" the Federal Farm Board must largely depend in supervising the biggest business in America.

Coöperating with the Federal Farm Board in every way consistent with our convictions, let us consider this important problem without prejudice, suggesting such policies and amendments as will be of real aid in placing farming on the same commercially sound basis as other industries. No elaborate machinery is required, only two major agencies—the Federal Farm Board and, for each standard farm product, a Commodity Marketing Board. Farming should be treated as an industry; its marketing as a business enterprise, adopting modern methods and conducted in accordance with the most advanced commercial practices. Each commodity or similar groups must be considered as a whole. Any other policy would be futile.

### 4,000,000 Farmers Not Members of Coöperatives

The present law deals entirely with coöperatives. There are 12,500 farm coöperatives in this country now, with 2,000,000 members. Under the plan which I propose and have urged for many years, no coöperative need lose its identity or disrupt its organization. By combining they would form component parts of their respective national commodity marketing agencies, increasing their effectiveness and multiplying their membership. Four million farmers, however, do not belong to any coöperative—twice as many as the total coöperative membership. The new law makes no provision for them. President Hoover has said, "The traditional coöperative is not a solution." Compelling farmers to join them would not solve the problem. In some states not 10 per cent belong to any coöperatives. These millions outside who have no vocal "leaders" form the largest element and the one in greatest need, a large proportion being tenant farmers, living from hand to mouth. Any plan that does not include them is not half effective.

### GREAT NATION-WIDE COMMODITY MARKETING ORGANIZATIONS REQUIRED

Farmers are beginning to realize the need of organizations big and powerful enough to fight for their interests, able to market effectively and give results which they can count in dollars and cents. Unless that principle is laid down millions will be wasted and confusion worse confounded. How such a system can be created and made effective has been my thought and study for twenty years. For the first time in history farming has been signally recognized by a special session of Congress. From the strong appeal made by the Institute of Public Affairs, I construe your call to be one for an earnest effort to solve the predominating problem before the American people, and I shall so treat it.

Assembled under the auspices of the University of Virginia, let us endeavor to formulate the basic principles of a plan that will in reality place farming on a commercial level with other industries, none of which equal it in property values or importance to the consuming masses. Let us be specific, determined to place this vital question before the people clearly, with definite recommendations to the Federal Board and

Congress, to farmers and the thinking men and women
who depend upon that industry for their daily bread.
Let us get away from the old political schemes and lay
down the principles of New Farm Economics. To do so
we must take a long and revolutionary step, abandon-
ing the old threadbare policies and practices that have
prevailed, with increasing hardship on farmers, for
more than fifty years. In doing so we must awaken to
the fact that we are in a period of huge combinations,
some of them world-wide, which are rapidly absorbing
and changing the entire character of American commerce, finance and industry. Like creeping paralysis
this is sucking the life blood from the farming industry
through control of finished products made from farm
raw materials.

### Immense Combines and Mergers in Farm Products Being Formed

Big Business, under present day conditions, is
originated, operated, merged, and capitalized through
combinations. Farming, the largest of them all, is not
organized under control of its producers, and is left
open to exploitation. In this period of unprecedented
prosperity, farm values have declined in ten years from
$79,000,000,000 to $57,500,000,000, due to the fact
that farming is not commercialized under combined organizations, is not commercially capitalized, and has no
selling or distributing system by which each standard
commodity would be handled by its own separate Marketing Board, whose duty it would be to look after the
producers' interests in every respect.

Never before has financial attention of towering strength been directed so strongly under colossal combinations to merchandising finished farm products. This makes it mandatory for farmers to combine in the same manner to meet these new economic conditions which, if not firmly combated, mean increased distress to American farmers. Powerful combinations have been and are constantly being formed controlling bread, flour, meats, dairy products, breakfast cereals and all standard foods. Makers of farm machinery, steel and wire, fertilizers and other manufactures and materials have long controlled nearly everything the farmer has to buy. New combines are now reaching out to control everything he has to sell, through control of the finished product manufactured from his raw material. As an example of what is becoming a daily occurrence—one merger with a capital of $430,000,000 was recently announced; another monster food company is being formed with hundreds of millions. One corporation has recently acquired 54 dairy plants in a dozen states, another has taken over dairy companies in nearly half the Union. In the last three years financial combinations for control of food supply aggregate more than $2,000,000,000—four times as great as the entire appropriations of $500,000,000 to provide for one-third of our farmers, leaving two-thirds at the mercy of gigantic corporations. In this regard, the law as it stands is inadequate.

Large corporations in future will not be confined to non-perishables, but are beginning to handle perishable foods, which can be utilized advantageously for all perishable farm products. But producers of perishables must also be organized under Commodity Boards combining similar products, under which I can see much benefit. To illustrate, I am giving extracts from a letter I have just received, but cannot at this time divulge the names of the promoters except to say that they are responsible and will carry out their intentions in good faith:

I wish to advise that there is now in the state of formation a new corporation, involving an initial capital of ten to fifteen million dollars, which with the equipment and other properties involved will aggregate a total capital of twenty-five million dollars or more, and with ample provision for further expansion.

The object of this corporation is the establishment and acquisition of probably fifty central distributing points in the United States, managed by trained men of many years of experience, for the purpose of dealing directly with the farms and guiding production as well as distribution, on a basis that will avoid gluts and overproduction.

It is proposed to place the business of farming on the same sound business basis that other commodities are being handled on today. It is this manner of merchandising which we intend to carry out and which we feel will prove convincing to the grower that we have reached a new era in the handling and distribution of farm products which is being participated in by some of the strongest financial interests of the country who are beginning to recognize its importance.

This is a long step in the right direction, and with producers so organized it would be of equal advantage to producers, transporters, and consumers, all on an equal basis. My prediction of twenty years ago, made in a speech at Dallas, Texas, is rapidly coming true, that "The time will come when producers, transporters, and consumers will work in harmony."

### FARMERS MUST FORM MARKETING COMBINES OF THEIR OWN

Farmers must organize big marketing combines of their own to meet the new conditions. The situation can be controlled only by farmers combining to sell through Commodity Marketing Boards.

When earnings increase largely, corporations, instead of paying 50 to 100 per cent dividends, double or triple their capital stock. Interest and dividends on this increased capital must be paid to their millions of stockholders. It is only human nature for them to buy raw material from farmers as cheaply as possible and sell for as much as the finished product will stand. That is good business. These mergers and combines have highly efficient selling and distributing systems. Legally organized, well entrenched, they are here to stay. To try to break them down legally or through legislation would be folly and would place us in the same category with the politicians.

Farmers organized under two simple amendments to the present Farm Law, enabling them to meet this condition which will be a growing menace to their business if allowed to proceed unchallenged, is the only remedy. They should have authority for—

1. Control of production so as to prevent unwieldy surpluses.

2. Control of distribution and marketing through Commodity Marketing Boards for each standard

product without cost to any other commodity or cost
to the Government except an initial loan for organization expenses including educational work. Farmers
have a fundamental advantage as first owners of the
raw material. But that is not effective unless they also
control its sale.

What is to be gained by politicians shouting from
the housetops that they will "place farming on a commercial level with other industries" when they provide
no effective means by which the farmers can organize
their marketing and business on an equal basis? The
law should be amended so as to enable producers to
form Commodity Marketing Boards with ample
authority to control production, distribution and sale of
their respective commodities. Farm Marketing Boards
should be established and conducted on as solid a business basis as the largest commercial combines, and be as
soundly financed.

### Essentials of Successful Farm Commodity Marketing

The essentials of a comprehensive, efficient Farm
Marketing System may be briefly stated:

Each standard commodity organized as a separate
independent commercial unit, under control of its producers, its general marketing directed by one central
Commodity Marketing Board.

Organizations to be nation-wide, embracing all co-
operatives and individual producers of the commodity.

Control of production, distribution and sale by
farmers' commodity marketing organizations.

No charge or expense imposed by one commodity on another and no expense to the Government except for loans for organization and initial capital.

Stabilizing prices at a fair figure to consumers to cover cost of production plus a reasonable profit.

Creating a marketing system big and efficient enough to attract the great mass of our 6,000,000 farmers.

While this plan is applicable to all standard farm commodities, I am going to use as illustrations two products which are daily quoted, bought and sold in this and foreign countries on a cash basis, cotton and wheat, therefore creating gilt-edge security and credit with financial institutions as safe as any other industrial loan.

## WHEAT AND COTTON: THE TWO GREAT "MONEY CROPS"

Eighty per cent of our wheat is produced in 14 states, though some wheat is grown in nearly every part of the country. Eighty per cent of our cotton is produced in 8 states, all but a few thousand bales in 14 states. Combined in great marketing associations covering the chief producing area, the growers can practically control these crops, if the present law is slightly modified to permit them to do so. A simple amendment to the new Farm Law enabling farmers to form their own Wheat or Cotton Marketing Board (the same applicable to other products) would be the beginning of solving the farm problem. The greatest results would, of course, come from the higher stabilized prices which efficient marketing boards would obtain. But these boards would earn substantial profits on their own account and, by building up reserves, be able in a few years to finance their operations with their own resources, without depending on Government aid. Financial institutions, big and little, would extend credit as freely on wheat and cotton as on any other raw material for manufacturing, if held by legally constituted Marketing Boards operating under Federal authority.

### COTTON—THE SOUTH'S GREAT MONOPOLY

In cotton the South has a virtual monopoly. Our planters could always get profitable prices under a marketing board limiting production to meet and not exceed the world's demands. By combining on a big scale, under Federal authority, cotton growers can control their marketing and stabilize prices at a profitable figure, bringing hundreds of millions increased income annually to farmers of the Cotton States, increasing their debt paying ability and purchasing power accordingly.

### MOVING RAPIDLY TOWARD COMBINED MARKETING

Farmers are moving rapidly toward that end in spite of the existing handicaps. Years ago when I first urged wheat and cotton growers to form great central marketing organizations, many critics said it was impracticable; that you could never induce farmers or the various farm organizations to "get together." The same objection was raised only a year ago when I urged the various wheat coöperatives to combine in one central marketing agency, submitting a comprehensive

plan for marketing the American wheat crop. Some
said it could not be done. Now they are combining to
form a large grain marketing corporation on the same
general lines that I urged, but it does not cover the
scope of the plan I proposed.

When the law is so amended as to permit real crop
control, the movement will extend rapidly to other
commodities. There are 17 standard farm commodities
and more than 80 food products produced on the farm,
many of which can derive no advantage from the
present law. It was gratifying to me, of course, to see
Congress setting forth in its declaration of policy the
basic principle of farmer-owned and farmer-controlled
organizations which I have so long advocated. But, in
failing to provide for Commodity Marketing Boards
with ample authority, the House and Senate fell short
of furnishing the means for attaining the desired results.

### Control of Production is Vital

Huge surpluses overwhelm both wheat and cotton
growers, as well as producers of other products, breaking prices to ruinous figures. Control that incubus and
prices can readily be stabilized. Controlling production
is as important as distribution and marketing. They go
together. Limiting planted acreage is the one practicable method, allotting acreage to be planted on the
basis of the average for the previous five years as
shown by Department of Agriculture reports, each
state and district being assigned its quota. In years
of large yield there might be an excess of, say, 100,-

000,000 bushels of wheat or 1,000,000 bales of cotton.
If so, these could be carried over on a margin of 20
per cent. In wheat at $1.50 a bushel, this would in-
volve $38,000,000; in cotton at 25 cents a pound, $25,-
000,000, above the 80 per cent credit which would be
obtainable through ordinary banking channels, if and
when controlled acreage and regulated marketing are
established by authority of Congress. By giving these
commodities an established credit, all financial institutions will feel as safe in extending credit on as good
terms as they would on oil or steel.

Some will argue that when wheat and cotton are
firmly held around these prices, the growers will increase their acreage and produce larger surpluses than
ever. That could be avoided, under amendments to the
Federal Farm Law, by granting Wheat and Cotton Marketing Boards authority, under the Federal Farm Board,
to control all interstate and foreign shipments of these
commodities under similar authority to that now exercised by the Interstate Commerce Commission over interstate and foreign freight rates. Growers or specu-
lators would find they could not ship wheat or cotton
from one state to another without the consent of the
Wheat or Cotton Marketing Boards, and farmers finding they were obtaining profitable rather than losing
prices, would plant according to the Marketing Boards'
instructions. The Marketing Boards could, further-
more, refuse to handle the interstate shipments of
those who exceed the acreage allotted them. Thus there
would be two powerful checks against overplanting.

## SPECULATION VS. SOUND BUSINESS PRACTICE

Speculation is prominent in the present law. Stabilization corporations are authorized to buy in vast quantities when prices are low, storing and carrying over huge surpluses with all the risks and hazards that involves. If they win, 75 per cent of the profits goes into a reserve fund until that fund is considered ample to cover possible losses. From the remainder, so-called "patronage dividends" may be paid. The farmer gets what is left—if any. If they lose, who loses? The United States Government is exempt. Stockholders are not subject to assessment. Any losses must be made up by further loans from the Federal revolving fund. When that is exhausted, what will you have? Either a bankrupt Federal Board or further appropriations of the taxpayers' money with no relief to the farmers. Without some definite check on production, which the present law does not provide, this would inevitably stimulate, not discourage, overproduction. Temporary surpluses, due to larger yields, are unavoidable. But no power on earth can hold up prices indefinitely in the face of constantly mounting surpluses. The whole scheme of stabilization would fall of its own weight, with heavy losses.

Marketing on sound business principles, preventing unwieldy surpluses through crop control, is the basis of the plan I propose, not speculation. Stabilization is also required, but is based on actual values and consumer demands. One is a Government gamble. The other is a business undertaking, involving only ordinary commercial risks. That is a basic difference. To put farming permanently on a self sustaining and paying basis, there must be a marketing control plan by which the six million farmers of this country can form a genuinely efficient nation-wide marketing system of their own. Lacking such a provision, the present scheme seems to me top heavy, cumbersome—a lofty structure with no firm foundation. A few simple amendments enabling farmers to organize for marketing national in scope forming their own Commodity Marketing Boards, would, in my opinion, strengthen the law, provide a proper basis for organization and marketing and enable the Federal Farm Board to carry into effect on a broad scale the purposes for which a majority of farmers believed it was created.

### A National Chamber to Represent Farming

Just one more suggestion, which I will leave with you. Nothing of permanent value to the farming industry can be accomplished except through a permanent organized body. One great need is for a national Chamber of Agriculture, representing the farming interests as ably and effectively as the United States Chamber of Commerce represents commerce, industry and finance. I have frequently pointed out the desirability of such a body and at the beginning of this year addressed a letter making the suggestion to hundreds of Chambers of Commerce throughout the United States. The response was cordial, showing the willingness of business men to aid the farmers in solving their business problems. I followed this up by an address under the auspices of the American Chamber of Agriculture on June 11th, in Washington.

The "American Chamber of Agriculture" was organized in Atlanta last January by leading farmers of the South. Men of high standing were named as its directors and advisers, with Col. W. C. Chase as executive vice president—Governor Hardeman, Ex-Senator Hoke Smith, Col. Samuel Tate and others of Georgia; Ex-Governor McLean and Hugh McRae of North Carolina; Governor Byrd and other leading Virginians, and such national figures as former Governor Lowden of Illinois and Hon. R. W. Dunlap, Assistant Secretary of Agriculture.

The Chamber of Agriculture should embrace all the farming interests of the country, including farm owners and tenants, whether members or non-members of other organizations. Above all things it should be nonpartisan, kept free of politics, not be used for any political or selfish purpose. Any Chamber that is instituted with the idea of advancing political fortunes or the interests of leaders or particular organizations cannot command public confidence and is destined to failure. It would be unfortunate and disastrous for any group to subject this great problem to petty politics. Voluntary organizations formed for the public good cannot, however, serve their purposes without funds to defray expenses. With an active executive secretary, familiar with the work of raising funds, the money to organize and carry on can be obtained.

I should say that $100,000 should be provided for a three-year campaign. The Chamber would be justified in starting with $50,000, but with nothing less. I am certain that ten men at least can be found who will subscribe $5,000 each, payable in twelve quarterly payments in three years. And I am equally sure that 100 founder members will willingly subscribe from $250 to $1,000 each, to be paid in three years in quarterly payments. With an experienced organizing secretary, from 500,000 to a million farmers will enroll when they understand that the object of the Chamber is unselfishly to aid them in building up their business on a sound, enduring basis and establishing economic freedom for American farmers. To assure the Chamber's future and prevent it from falling under the domination of selfish or political influences, it should be organized under an alternating system of electing directors.

Unless business men and women take hold of this predominating farm problem in a determined, organized effort, I fear for the country's future. If this forum under the auspices of the University of Virginia will present a well thought out plan for restoring America's farm citizenship, establishing their economic freedom and restoring them from their bankrupt condition to prosperity on an equality with other industries, history will record it as a greater deed than that of Thomas Jefferson in his fight for democracy against bureaucracy. Jefferson fought for a high principle with a sparse population. Your fight is for justice against a powerful organized dealer population with almost unbounded wealth at their command. Enabling our six million farmers to organize for their own protection and place their industry on a solid and profitable business basis will have more far-reaching effects than any other movement of our generation.

# INDEX

# THE UNIVERSITY OF NORTH CAROLINA
## SOCIAL STUDY SERIES

UNDER THE GENERAL EDITORSHIP OF HOWARD W. ODUM. BOOKS MARKED WITH * PUBLISHED IN COÖPERATION WITH THE INSTITUTE FOR RESEARCH IN SOCIAL SCIENCE

(See next page)

*The University of North Carolina Press, Chapel Hill, N. C.; The Baker and Taylor Co., New York; Oxford University Press, London; The Maruzen Company, Tokyo; Edward Evans & Sons, Ltd., Shanghai.*

9 781469 613604